NORTH KOREA IN 100 FACTS

RUTH ANN MONTI

AMBERLEY

Many thanks to Yvonne Gee, who proofread each fact and whose research helped me understand the linguistic differences between Korean and Japanese kirin and Chinese qilin. Although some will disagree, I have concluded that unicorns don't exist, not even in North Korea.

I dedicate this book to my father, Milton Chinitz, whose national service fell during the Korean War years and included winter training along the very cold US–Canadian border. Thankfully, this particular unit remained stateside.

Ruth Ann Monti
Scottsdale, Arizona

First published 2019

Amberley Publishing
The Hill, Stroud
Gloucestershire, GL5 4EP

www.amberley-books.com

British Library Cataloguing in Publication Data.
A catalogue record for this book is available from the British Library.

ISBN 978 1 4456 8696 7 (paperback)
ISBN 978 1 4456 8697 4 (ebook)

Typeset in 10.5pt on 13pt Sabon.
Origination by Amberley Publishing.
Printed in the UK.

Contents

1. North Korea Is a Successful Hereditary Dictatorship

North Korea may be one of the poorest countries in the world but it's No. 1 in one area: it is the only hereditary dictatorship to last into a third generation.

The country, which calls itself by the ancient Korean name Choson, was established in 1945 by the Soviet Union after its Japanese occupiers were defeated in the Second World War. The US and Soviet Union agreed to divide the Korean Peninsula, with the northern part under Soviet protection and the southern section under the US's.

The country's first leader, Kim Il-sung, was an anti-Japanese guerrilla leader who later served as an officer in the Soviet Army and was put in charge of the Korean Communist Party. In 1948, he established a provisional Communist government in the newly created Democratic People's Republic of Korea. The following year, he was named chairman of the new Korean Workers' Party, which supplanted the Communist Party. In 1950, Kim invaded South Korea in an attempt to unify the peninsula under Communist rule. That resulted in a disastrous war for the North that continued until 1953, when both sides agreed to an armistice, but not an official peace, a situation that exists to this day. North Koreans, who are taught that the US and South Korea invaded their country, call the war the 'Fatherland Liberation War'.

During these years, Kim crushed all political opposition and created a personality cult which surpassed even that of his Soviet sponsor and role model Josef Stalin. As Kim consolidated power, he began ordering statues and portraits of himself to be placed in literally every public space around the country, and took the title of Suryong, or 'Great Leader'. He created an official autobiography in which he described defeating the Japanese and Americans almost entirely on his own.

In the 1960s, Kim began to link his son Kim Jong-il to his cult. Statues and portraits of the two Kims standing together became as ubiquitous as the father's single image had been, and stories about the younger Kim's genius began popping up. With criticisms about Mao's personality cult leaking into North Korea, Kim *pere* wanted to be sure his son would adhere to his vision to lead a completely submissive nation and decreed Kim Jong-il would be known as the 'Dear Leader'.

When Kim 'died' (officially, he isn't actually dead) in 1994, the stage was set for Kim Jong-il to take over. He really went overboard with dozens of nicknames including 'Saviour', 'Eternal General Secretary of the Party', and 'World Leader of the Twenty-first Century'.

As Kim Jong-il's health declined in the early twenty-first century (so much for titles), he ensured his favourite son, Kim Jong-un, was steadily promoted. Since his father's death in 2011, Kim Jong-un has been called 'Dear Respected Comrade', 'Supreme Leader', and 'Our Marshall'. He is firmly in place as North Korea's leader, where many believe he holds the same supernatural powers as his father and grandfather.

2. THE KOREAN PENINSULA WAS OCCUPIED BY JAPAN IN THE FIRST HALF OF THE TWENTIETH CENTURY

The Korean Peninsula became a Japanese protectorate in 1905 after the Great Korean Empire collapsed after a long and bitter history of intensive intrusions from Russia, China, and several Western nations.

Japan and Russia fought the Russo-Japanese War 1904–1905 over territorial ambitions in the area then called Manchuria, and Korea. Much of the war was fought on water and to everyone's surprise, Japan's navy defeated Russia's. The war formally ended with the Treaty of Portsmouth negotiated by US President Theodore Roosevelt, who was awarded the 1906 Nobel Peace Prize for his efforts. But as Blaine Harden notes, the treaty was really a trade-off to allow the US to continue its forays into the Philippines while ceding Korea to Japanese control.[1]

Japan forced Korea's sitting emperor, Gojong, to abdicate in 1907 in favour of his son Sunjong, who in turn abdicated in 1910, ending the Korean Empire, and was also the last of the Yi dynasty that dated from 1392.

Nearly 1 million Koreans immigrated to Japan after the First World War to fill labour shortages. During the Second World War, Japan conscripted 5.4 million Korean men and sent around 670,000 to work as forced labourers on its mainland, usually in mines, construction sites and military facilities. Japan did not draft Koreans into its military until 1944, when it accepted 200,000 men into the Imperial Army. Around 60,000 Koreans had died in Japan by the time it surrendered,

---

1 Harden, Blaine, *The Great Leader and the Fighter Pilot: a True Story about the Birth of Tyranny in North Korea* (Penguin Books, 2016), p.18.

including those sent to work at military sites in Hiroshima and Nagasaki where the US dropped the bomb.

By then, distrust between Koreans and Japanese ran high. The historian Gavan Daws wrote that Japanese soldiers were known to kill Korean labourers for fear that they would attack them in the event of an American invasion.[2] Millions more Koreans were sent to Manchuria, which Japan's Imperial Army had invaded in 1931. Others were forced to work in Japanese-owned factories in Korea. The number of Koreans who died working at home and in Manchuria during the war may be as high as 800,000.

Japan also kidnapped or lured hundreds of thousands of women from Korea and other Southeast Asian nations it occupied to serve as 'comfort women' to its soldiers during the Second World War. Yoshiaki Yoshimi, a professor at Chuo University in Tokyo, studied Imperial Army medical records of venereal diseases and discovered that 51 per cent of comfort women treated were Korean while 36 per cent came from China. This may be the best estimate about the origins of most of Japan's sex slaves that we have.

Japan's surrender in September 1945 ended its occupation of Korea. American forces arrived on the southern part of the peninsula while the Soviet Army stationed itself in the north.

---

2 Daws, Gavan, *Prisoners of the Japanese POWS of WWII in the Pacific* (William Morrow, 1995).

3. Kim Il-sung Grew Up with Protestant Influences and Support

Kim Il-sung may have banned traditional religion from South Korea but as a child and young man, Christians treated him pretty well and he was content enough to associate with them.

He was born 15 April 15 1912, in a small village near Pyongyang to parents who were still in their teens. He was given the name Kim Song-ju. As a child, Kim was raised in the Protestant faith many Koreans adhered to at the time; Pyongyang was sometimes called 'Korea's Jerusalem'. Bradley Martin writes in his extensive analysis of the Kim Dynasty that Kim's mother was thought to be a deaconess, although Kim later wrote that she went to church to relax and nap during services.

Kim's family moved to Jilin in China around 1920 with thousands of other Koreans to escape Japan's harsh rule in Korea as well as the famines that regularly swept the peninsula. (Japan did not invade the region until 1931.) His father died in 1926. As a teenager, Kim joined other youthful Korean nationalists and became familiar with the tenets of Communism.

Still, Martin writes, he remained 'very happy to deal with' a Methodist clergyman, Revd Sohn Jong-do, who was an active supporter of Korean independence and a friend of his late father. He played the organ in Sohn's church, and Sohn paid his school fees and hosted him at family holidays. Sohn's youngest son, who later emigrated to the US and became a pathologist, recalled Kim as a 'tall lad who smiled a lot'.[1]

---

1 Martin, Bradley K., *Under the Loving Care of the Fatherly Leader: North Korea and the Kim Dynasty* (Thomas Dunne Books, 2007), p. 71.

Kim was active with the Jilin Children's Association, which used the church for its meetings and helped them write and put on skits. In his memoirs, Kim says he tried to enlighten the children about religious trickery and instead fight for Korean independence. Dr Sohn, however, says Kim did not appear to be anti-religion and played the organ for church services. He believes his father, while not a Communist, indulged Kim because he was the son of a friend, was obviously very intelligent, and a likely future leader of the independent Korea so many hoped for.

Sohn and his family continued looking after Kim during his brief stint in a Jilin prison in 1929–30 for leading a pro-Soviet demonstration to invade Manchuria and free it of Japanese rule. They sent him care packages and Revd Sohn even offered a bribe to secure his release after he and other Communists resorted to a hunger strike. Kim was released in May 1930, largely because the local authorities believed he was too young to be much of a threat.

Sohn's support had to have some impact on Kim's outlook. He ended the preface to his memoirs on a rather spiritual note: 'Praying for the souls of the departed revolutionaries.'

4. KIM IL-SUNG DISTRUSTED CHINA AND THE USSR

Although China and the USSR were important backers of North Korea, Kim Il-sung had reason to distrust both nations. Manchurian Communists tried to execute him as a young man, while Stalin often held back his political ambitions.

As a young man in the late 1920s and early 1930s, Kim lived near the Korean border in China, which was eventually occupied by Japan, and he was part of an armed resistance. But local Communists, convinced that ethnic Korean residents and Korean resistance fighters were secretly conspiring with the Japanese, tortured and killed around 1,000 of them in a terrible event known as the Minsaengdan Incident.

Kim escaped execution when allies in the larger Chinese Communist Party intervened on his behalf. It also helped that he spoke Chinese and, as Blaine Harden notes, was thought to be too young at twenty-two to be a spy. China's Communists also put a stop to the massacre, and Kim formed a guerrilla band of Korean ex-prisoners. They famously raided local prisons to free other Koreans and burned their prison records.

Kim became something of a guerrilla folk hero in the late 1930s after he led a raid on the border town of Pochonbo, killing some Japanese police officers and burning several government buildings. The Japanese authorities gave him further credibility by naming him Public Enemy No. 1. News of the raid was reported around the globe, including in the USSR and Europe.

The Japanese redoubled their efforts to regain control in occupied China and Kim lived on the run for a few years, barely surviving harsh winters with little food and sustenance. By 1940, many of his guerrillas were dead or in Japanese prisons. A small band followed him to escape into the USSR, where they were arrested in Vladivostok.

When Stalin found out Kim had been arrested, he saw a potentially useful tool in Korea. Once his health stabilised, Kim was sent to an infantry officers' school where he stayed for two years. He was then sent to a military base in Khabarovsk, around 20 miles from the Chinese border, with the rank of captain. There, he married one of his followers, Kim Jong-suk, who followed him into the USSR upon her release from a Japanese prison. Their son, Kim Jong-il, was born in Khabarovsk.

Kim worked hard to impress his Soviet Army superiors. While he wasn't the highest-ranking Korean at the base, he was, Harden says, the most influential,[1] probably due to his transition from guerrilla fighter to a well-trained officer. Contrary to North Korean history books, he wasn't granted a hero's welcome back home when he returned to Korea after Japan's surrender. In fact, he wasn't named Korea's leader until the Soviet's initial choice, Cho Man-sik, refused to join the Communist Party or agree to be anyone's puppet – laying out Kim's first big challenge.

1 Harden, *The Great Leader and the Fighter Pilot*, p.33.

5. Cho Man-sik Might Have Led One Korea

Cho Man-sik was a popular independence leader in Korea during Japanese rule and in the years following the Second World War. He might have been the first leader of a unified Korea.

Born in present-day North Korea in 1883, Cho was raised in a traditional Confucian style. As a young man, he was apparently a pretty rowdy fellow until he became a Protestant. He left Korea in 1908 to study law in Japan, where he encountered and embraced Gandhi's teachings about non-violent resistance.

After graduating from law school in 1913, Cho returned to Korea and served as a principal at a mission school that became a base for Korean independence. He helped establish new schools and championed a campaign to restore Korean dignity and self-determination. He was one of the leaders of the massive March 1st Movement when 2 million Koreans called for independence on 1 March 1919. He was arrested and jailed for a short time.

In 1922, Cho founded the Korean Products Promotion Society to spur a cultural reawakening by encouraging Koreans to buy Korean-made products, eat traditional foods, and aspire to self-determination. Cho himself gave up Western clothing and wore the traditional hanbok – a kind of robe. He lived 'like a peasant', according to an essay by Kenneth Wells of the Australian National University, and gained respect even from opponents who questioned his Christian practices. His humble lifestyle and devotion to non-violence led people to call him 'Korea's Gandhi'.[1]

---

1 Wells, Kenneth. 'The Rationale of Korean Economic Nationalism Under Japanese Control.' *Modern Asian Studies*, (vol. 19, no. 4, 1985), http://bit.ly/2NlJAQ5.

Just before Japan surrendered to US forces, Cho formed the Provisional People's Committee for the Five Provinces, a solidly anti-Communist group. Shortly after they reached Pyongyang, the Soviets approached him to discuss his role in the emerging North Korean state. But Cho disliked Communism (he was, after all, a religious Protestant) and wanted far more autonomy than the Soviets would allow. As a nationalist, he refused to accept a divided Korea.

Things really fell apart when the Soviets asked Kim Il-sung to bring Cho to an expensive restaurant and brothel in a last-ditch effort to persuade him to co-operate. Not surprisingly, this failed. Cho reorganised his party into the Democratic Party of Korea, which quickly fell under Soviet influence.

His fate was sealed when he refused to endorse the Moscow Conference, which created a five-year agreement for an international trusteeship of Korea before it could become an independent state. The frustrated Soviets arrested him in 1946, and imprisoned him at a Pyongyang hotel. He was on the 1948 ballot for North Korea's vice presidency, but won just ten votes in the National Assembly.

At some point, Cho was taken to a prison in Pyongyang. Witnesses say he was executed with around 500 other prisoners by the North Korean Army on 18 October 1950, just as the Korean War broke out. He was buried in a mass grave.

6. KIM IL-SUNG FLATTERED THE SOVIETS INTO NAMING HIM NORTH KOREA'S LEADER

As soon as he landed in North Korea in the fall of 1945, Kim began preparing his future. He told his soldiers to keep a low profile, stay sober, and if asked, to tell people they were preparing for the 'grand arrival' of Kim Il-sung, Harden writes. Meanwhile, he began a charm offensive on local Soviet generals, arranging 'boozy banquets' for them, complete with prostitutes.[1] In return, they agreed to place his friends in security posts. It didn't take long for Kim to have a spy in nearly every police department and military base.

Once the Soviets gave up on Cho Man-sik, they installed Kim as the nation's new leader in front of tens of thousands of people in Pyongyang. They bungled his introduction by writing a very ideological speech for him about Marxism, which few Koreans understood. Worse, Harden notes, most of the crowd thought the Kim they saw was a fake; based on the stories they had heard about him, they expected a more mature leader and instead found themselves watching a 'callow young man', one observer recalled.[2] To top it all off, in an attempt to build up his scrawny physical stature, the Soviets dressed him in a Western-style suit a size too small.

This could have backfired badly but for the efficiency of the Soviet propaganda machine that quickly kicked in for damage control and gave Kim an appreciation for state-sponsored hype. His official biography built up his status as a folk hero. Billboards went up of Kim wearing a Mao suit and with a fuller face than the one he presented at his installation ceremony.

Kim's public relations offensive began around a month later with a visit to the North Korean/Manchurian border

---

1 Harden, *The Great Leader and the Fighter Pilot*, p. 34.
2 Ibid, pp. 34–35.

town of Sinuiju. The city had been the site of the nation's largest anti-Communist demonstration, led by students and Christian activists who surrounded several Communist Party buildings. This action was answered by air and ground attacks from Soviet soldiers and Korean Communists. Around 100 students were killed and 700 wounded, later followed by Red Army soldiers looting the city. The news spread and spurred anti-Communist demonstrations in other Korean cities.

Using his stature as a Korean patriot, Kim persuaded an end to the demonstrations. He characterised the attacks as the work of 'fake Communists' and reactionaries. And instead of scolding the demonstrators for their anti-Communist proclamations, he just said they were naïve. In fact, many survivors were later drafted into an elite Peace Preservation Officers' School established in Sinuiju.

After Sinuiju, Kim embarked on his first listening and advice tour throughout the country that became one of the hallmarks of North Korea's leaders. Newspapers praised his common touch. Meanwhile, he worked to build up a 100,000-man Korean army he intended to use to drive out the US from South Korea and unify the peninsula.

7. EVERYONE WANTED A WAR BUT ONLY KIM WANTED TO FIGHT

The Soviet Union left the Korean peninsula in September 1948 after establishing the Democratic People's Republic of North Korea. In the South, the Western-backed Republic of Korea had been proclaimed a few months earlier.

Kim's goal was to unite the peninsula. He learned from captured South Korean soldiers that their army was much weaker than the North's; in his opinion, the time was right to strike even with the continued presence of US troops. Still, an invasion of the South would require some anti-Western muscle and he began actively campaigning to get support from the two pre-eminent Communist nations: China and the USSR.

He visited the leaders of both nations in 1950. First, he travelled to Moscow in May, where Stalin made it clear he wouldn't openly support an invasion. He preferred to draw China into a war against the US, in the role of a Soviet client state. He pledged to continue arming the North Korean Army but told Kim he would end this support if he invaded the South without China's assent. Kim, who had seen how the Chinese could treat Koreans (see Fact 4), was not convinced. He was certain the US, who left China as its own civil war began, would not risk a war with a unified China.

Most of all, Kim was a nationalist and did not want someone else to direct the invasion. So he asked for and got a meeting with Mao. He knew Mao was grateful to North Korean Communists who fought with him against the Chinese nationalist Chiang Kai-shek, and Kim had shared with him intelligence about Soviet problems in North Korea. Earlier, Mao had even gone so far as to pledge stealth support and send soldiers for an invasion. 'We all have black hair, no one can tell the difference.'[1]

But Mao found Kim an annoying person who was too dogmatic and aggressive, a surprising charge from the man who would lead the Great Leap Forward a few years later. Worse, Mao saw Stalin's advice as a conditional 'yes' to invade the South at a time when he was preparing to invade Taiwan to unify *his* nation. He sent his premier and foreign minister Zhou Enlai to the USSR to demand an explanation. Stalin blithely explained that 'things change'.[2] The Chinese and Korean comrades should work out final details and if China disagreed on an invasion, it could be postponed.

This was a thinly veiled threat to withdraw aid the USSR was providing to help China modernise. Mao reluctantly contacted Kim to support unification but warned that the US, possibly with Japan, might start a bloody and protracted war. Kim disagreed: the Japanese wouldn't dare return and the US had already ducked a war in the region.

With both leaders' consent, Kim invaded South Korea on 25 June 1950.

---

1 Shen, Zhihua, *Mao, Stalin, and the Korean War: Trilateral Communist Relations in the 1950s.* 2012, p. 126.
2 Ibid.

8. THE USSR AND CHINA MADE NORTH KOREA DISAPPEAR FOR A DAY

Both the USSR and China played some serious mind games with North Korea after the 1950 invasion.

North Korea initially overpowered the South. Within three days, Kim was in Seoul while most of the South Korean Army fell apart. US troops from Japan were inexperienced, especially compared to the North Korean veterans of the Chinese Civil War. Half the force was killed, wounded, or taken prisoner. Even its commander, General William F. Dean, got lost in his Jeep and was taken as a Prisoner of War.

Things changed with the arrival of the newly created US Air Force. After two months, the USAF had levelled most North Korean cities and ran out of targets. Stalin suggested to Mao it was time for China to send in troops. Mao reluctantly agreed and authorised a volunteer force to send to Korea with a condition: the USSR had to provide air cover.

On 11 October, the following events occurred:

> Stalin refused to commit to air cover, so Mao rescinded his commitment to send ground troops.
>
> Stalin ordered Kim to retreat, which he did, even asking a Soviet envoy for an evacuation plan. He told his closest associates to prepare to retreat into Manchuria where they could try to re-establish their old guerrilla army.
>
> Without support from the two Communist powers, North Korea ceased to exist.

A day later, Mao changed his mind and decided to send his volunteer force. Kim cancelled his plans to abandon ship and North Korea was essentially re-created.

9. THE US DROPPED SO MANY BOMBS ON NORTH KOREA EVEN GENERAL MACARTHUR WAS HORRIFIED

Before the Chinese joined their North Korean comrades, the new but powerful US Air Force dropped only conventional bombs on the North. That changed as Mao's volunteers drove back US soldiers.

Up to that point, the US held back from using napalm as it had done in Japan in 1944 and 1945, before it dropped the two atomic bombs. During that time, sixty-six Japanese cities were bombed with napalm, which killed 100,000 in Tokyo alone.

After the Chinese strengthened the North Koreans' position, political hesitancy in Washington was set aside as the Air Force went ahead with a devastating bombing campaign in November 1950, despite the very thorough bombings that had already wiped out most of North Korea's cities. The Air Force turned to other targets, such as dams that provided electricity and irrigation, and farmland, to bring utter devastation to the countryside as well as cities.

Napalm is a sticky gel that destroys buildings and skin. Its use in Vietnam in the 1960s was widely photographed and reported, fuelling (if you pardon the expression) worldwide demonstrations against the US-led war there. It probably helped persuade the majority of Americans to oppose the war as well as leading to the US's eventual withdrawal from Vietnam. But in 1950, the Korean War (or police action, as the US Congress termed it) was barely reported, unlike Vietnam. Until recently, the war was called 'America's Forgotten War'. And at the time, napalm wasn't in most Americans' vocabulary.

In 2015, an article in the *Washington Post* recounted a 1984 interview the Office of Air Force History conducted with US Air Force General Curtis LeMay. The Air Force,

LeMay said, killed around 20 per cent of the North Korean population (perhaps three million people) during the Korean War.[1] Most of it was done between November 1950 and January 1951, when the US dropped 40 per cent of all its bombs and two-thirds of the napalm – 32,000 tons – used during the entire three years of active war.

General Douglas MacArthur, the Second World War hero of the Pacific Theatre and to whom Japan surrendered, was placed in charge of the United Nations Command for South Korean troops. And although he no doubt approved the bombing orders, he later testified to the US Senate's Armed Services and Foreign Relations Committees about how shaken he had been by the devastation in North Korea.

'I have seen, I guess, as much blood and disaster as any living man, and it just curdled my stomach,' he testified. 'After I looked at that wreckage and those thousands of women and children and everything, I vomited.'[2] By then, President Harry S. Truman had fired MacArthur, with the full backing of his other military commanders, for ignoring Truman's orders against preparing for an invasion of China.

---

1 Harden, Blaine. 'The US War Crime North Korea Won't Forget.' *The Washington Post*, 15 Feb. 2015, https://wapo.st/2oeeIWM.
2 Harden, *The Great Leader and the Fighter Pilot*, p. 96.

10. North Korea's Youngest Pilot during the Korean War Defected Shortly after the Truce

On 21 September 1953, a few months after the Korean War ended in a truce, a North Korean fighter pilot named No Kum-sok landed his Soviet-made MiG-15bis jet at Kimpo Air Force base near Seoul, which housed the US Air Force's 398th Bomber Wing.

No was just twenty-one and the youngest fighter pilot for North Korea. At age seventeen he had been accepted into North Korea's naval academy on his second try, in which he omitted key facts about his family background. He assumed the US would defeat Kim; his goal was to ride out the war in the academy and move to the States.

Writing about No in his book *The Great Leader and the Fighter Pilot*, Blaine Harden tells a fascinating story. No came from a Catholic family; his father had worked for a Japanese company. He disguised his solidly anti-Communist sentiments by playing the part of an enthusiastic Communist and earning top grades in Soviet Communist Party history – the one class he recognised really mattered for him to succeed.

He was also extremely clever. As he watched a group of select fellow students undergo an unusual workout, he realised they were being tested for their potential to fly planes. He immediately volunteered to take the test and easily passed. He was sent to a Chinese Air Force base near the North Korean border where he was taught by Chinese and Soviet instructors to fly bombers. He became an elite, if very cautious, bomber pilot and one of a small group trained to fly MiGs, the best fighter jet in the Soviet fleet.

Two things helped No get by: his ability to play the dutiful Communist (he even started a base newspaper) and his fluency in Russian, thanks to a change in school curriculum that replaced English classes with Russian. Along the way, he waited for the perfect time to defect. By the time the war ended in a truce, he had learned that his mother had escaped to South Korea and realised he would probably be denounced for this. His opportunity came when the MiGs were smuggled out of China and into North Korea on Kim Il-sung's order.

No finally defected during a routine training run. As he approached the Kimpo base, he rocked his plane's wings back and forth – a sign of friendliness – and fired coloured flares to indicate an emergency landing. Most significantly, he landed the plane with the wind – against normal practice. To his amazement, the US personnel there didn't notice his jet until he actually landed it. 'It's a goddamn MiG!' a pilot who had just landed yelled over the radio as the two planes passed one another on the runway. Anti-aircraft gunners stationed on either side of the runway hesitated to fire, lest they hit each other.

No parked between two Sabre jets jumped out of the cockpit, and promptly destroyed the plane's framed photo of Kim Il-sung.

11. 'Operation Moolah' Failed to Persuade Russians and North Koreans to Defect during the Korean War

Fifteen days after Josef Stalin died and a few months before the Korean War truce, the US military launched an unusual campaign in the war zone: Operation Moolah, which offered $100,000 (£77,900) to anyone who delivered a MiG to them. Today, this would be worth close to $1 million (£779,000).

Two different parties claimed to come up with this idea: the Korea bureau chief of a now-defunct news service, and the US Air Force psychological warfare unit. Both thought that ambitious pilots would want the chance to defect and 'free themselves from the vicious whip of Communism'.[1] The initial idea was to spread, by word of mouth throughout Korea, that the US would pay a reward for any pilot from any nation who would defect with a MiG. Then *The Washington Post* got hold of the story and reported it under the headline 'General Mark Clark Offers $100,000 for Russian Jet.' (Clark commanded the US Far East forces.)

The scheme was put in place just as armistice talks began. US pilots dropped leaflets advertising the offer in Russian, Korean, Mandarin and Cantonese from B-29 bombers flying over the Yalu River. Fourteen radio stations in South Korea and Japan also broadcast it for around a week; Clark later said Russian broadcasts were jammed. The Soviets grounded their best pilots for the duration, leading to a loss of 165 additional MiGs.

No pilot came forward. The defector pilot No Kum-sok told Blaine Harden the messages didn't reach them because they were not in the Yalu River region where the leaflets were dropped and their base was out of broadcast range.

---

1 Harden, *The Great Leader and the Fighter Pilot*, p. 152.

Even if they had had heard about the offer over the radio, the pilots wouldn't have taken it seriously and anyway, they had no concept of what $100,000 was worth. The promise of a good job in the US, he said, would have been a more tempting offer.

President Dwight D. Eisenhower, himself a former general, hated Operation Moolah from the start. He worried about the ethics of stealing a MiG jet and bribing pilots. Once No defected, he hoped that particular pilot would reject the money.

He didn't. Eight months after he defected No agreed to a CIA-directed publicity stunt where he supposedly deposited the 'moolah' at Riggs Bank in Washington in a trust fund to help pay for his education and support his mother in South Korea. It took some time for him to believe the trust wasn't some kind of trick. It did come in handy when he enrolled at the University of Delaware to study aeronautical engineering in the autumn of 1954. By then he had had enough: whenever he was asked about the money, No lived up to his name and replied 'No comment.' Later, he changed his name to Kenneth R. Rowe.

12. China Contributed the Bulk of Reconstruction Support for North Korea

Kim Il-sung, Blaine Harden notes, had a real genius for gathering strength from failure, even (and perhaps especially) his own. The war, which he had started with China's clear disapproval and mixed messages from Stalin, left North Korea utterly devastated thanks to a 'back to the Stone Age' bombing campaign from the United States.

Kim played up his country's destruction, all but demanding aid from the USSR, China, and other socialist nations. North Korea, he argued, paid a heavy price to support Communist ideals and they were owed! As a result of these appeals, Harden says, North Korea 'vacuumed up more aid from socialist nations' than any other country, a record that stands to this day.[1] The new leaders of the Soviet Union may have been somewhat vulnerable to exploitation; many believed Stalin's carrot and stick tactics prolonged the war.

China, which was still in many ways a developing nation, was most generous. Its contribution was one-third larger than the total from the Soviet Union and other socialist nations.[2] Mao, who really disliked Kim, never forgot the Korean Communist volunteers who fought with him against the Japanese and later during China's civil war. 'The Korean people are brave,' he told a delegation of North Koreans visiting Beijing in November 1953, adding:

> They can handle suffering; they are courageous ... disciplined ... not afraid of hardship. We cannot match them in these respects. We should learn [from their example]... The Chinese

---

1 Harden, *The Great Leader and the Fighter Pilot*, p. 162.
2 Zhihua, Shen and Yafeng Xia, *China and the Post-war Reconstruction of North Korea, 1953–1961* (Woodrow Wilson International Center for Scholars, 2012), http://bit.ly/2P8C2k4, p. 7.

People's Volunteer Army and the Korean People's Army, as well as the people of Korea, struggled together and achieved victory together; assistance was mutual.[3]

China cancelled North Korea's war debt and provided funds to repair the country's transportation infrastructure and import grain. It also:

Took in more than 22,700 Korean child refugees

Discounted payments for Chinese experts helping rebuild North korea

Trained Korean mechanics and technicians at no cost (other than lodging and travel expenses) and gave them the same access as their Chinese counterparts

Provided free tuition and lodging to Korean students in China.

The Soviet Union offered similar on-site experts, as well as training and education in the USSR, but charged far higher rates.

So why was China so generous, particularly at a time when it needed to rebuild its own infrastructure? One explanation is that China wanted Korea in its orbit, not the Soviet Union's. Another point of view offered by the historians Shen Zhihua and Yafeng Xia is that Chinese leaders, particularly Premier Zhou Enlai, recognised the damaged relationship between Chinese and North Korean civilians. Kim himself had experienced cultural prejudice from Chinese Communists during his youth and there were no doubt plenty of tensions between soldiers from both countries during the Korean War.[4]

---

3 Ibid., p. 39.
4 Ibid., p. 7.

13. North Korea Is in a Never-ending War

As a nation, North Korea has internalised the Korean War into its very identity.

The Korean War is not officially over; it's an armistice at the 38th parallel where American officers decided to divide the peninsula in 1945. Official North Korean history says 'American Imperialists' invaded the North on 15 June 1950 – exactly the opposite of what actually happened.

Much of North Korean propaganda is aimed at the United States, understandable given the awful destruction rained down on civilians during the active war period. North Korea has generally viewed the South as an accomplice to American imperialism, alternatively voicing sympathy and scorn.

North Korea has also engaged in terrorism against political leaders in the South:

> In 1968, North Korean commandoes were stopped just in time from assassinating the South's president, Park Chung-hee. His wife, Yuk Young-soo, was killed.
>
> In 1983, agents from the North planted a bomb in Myanmar where South Korean president Chun Doo-hwan was staying during an official visit. It exploded early and killed 21 people, including four of his cabinet members.
>
> In 1987, two agents planted a bomb on Korean Air Flight 858 from Baghdad to Seoul, killing all 115 aboard. A male agent later committed suicide; his female partner was captured and confessed.
>
> More information on this is in Fact 14.

Things changed in 2013, when the North faxed the South Korean Defence Ministry threatening a 'merciless retaliation without warning' after some anti-North demonstrations were reported in Seoul. The South, in turn, faxed back its own threat vowing 'resolute punishment' for any provocations. Considering the history, this is a dial-down.

14. North Korea Bombed a South Korean Airliner in an Attempt to Halt the 1988 Seoul Olympic Games

North Korea was responsible for the 29 November 1987 bombing of Korean Airlines flight 858 en route from Abu Dhabi in the United Arab Emirates to Seoul, which killed all 115 passengers and crew. The plane exploded over the Andaman Sea between the Bay of Bengal and Myanmar. The bomb's purpose was to derail the upcoming 1988 Summer Olympics in Seoul.

Two North Korean agents, Kim Seung-il and Kim Hyon-hui, planted a bomb in an overhead compartment during a scheduled stopover in Abu Dhabi before the plane went on to Seoul. They had been posing as father and daughter and travelled with fake Japanese passports around Europe, stopping in major cities for instructions. After planting the bomb, they left the plane and boarded a flight to Bahrain, where they planned to go on to Rome. But they were detained by officials during a stopover in Bahrain on 1 December after they seemed unable to answer basic questions such as 'why are you traveling with just carry-on luggage?' or 'why has your itinerary changed so much?' They determined the passports were forgeries and turned them over to South Korean agents.

Kim Seung-il asked if he could smoke, and reached for a cigarette. His partner asked for one, too. Both cigarettes contained cyanide. As Kim Seung-il went into convulsions, a quick-thinking police officer hit Kim Hyon-hui's arm, preventing her from committing suicide; she bit enough cyanide only to lose consciousness. Her companion died shortly afterwards in hospital. She was sent to Seoul and arrived on 15 December, the day before a presidential election was held in South Korea.

Photos of Kim arriving in Seoul show her mouth taped and being supported by several agents. In Seoul, she insisted she was a Chinese orphan from the north and that her companion had adopted her. However, she only spoke Cantonese, a southern dialect. She was apparently broken after several trips inside Seoul, which she had been told all her life was a poor and corrupt city. After eight days, she confessed and provided a key detail: the bombing was personally ordered by Kim Il-sung and that she had been removed from university for special training to be part of the plot, which was intended to disrupt the Olympics and the presidential election.

Kim was the daughter of a career diplomat and had lived with her family in Cuba for a few years. After returning to North Korea, she worked as an actress and appeared in its first Technicolor film. She attended Kim Il-sung University and transferred to the Pyongyang Foreign Language College to study Japanese. From there, she was recruited for the Reconnaissance General Bureau, the North Korean spy agency.

Kim was sentenced to death but South Korea's President Roh Tae-woo pardoned her, citing her brainwashed life. She has since married a South Korean, provides news analysis, and writes books; proceeds go to the families of KAL 858 victims.

15. The DMZ is the Most Heavily Guarded Border in the World

The United States and Canada have shared the world's oldest undefended border since 1846, when the US and Great Britain agreed after several decades to use the 49th parallel. Y'all also agreed not to invade us again like you did in 1812 when you burned down the Executive Mansion in Washington DC, forcing us to paint it white and imaginatively rename it The White House.

The Korean Demilitarised Zone falls on the other side of the spectrum as the most heavily guarded and dangerous border in the world. It's been largely quiet since it was established in 1953, aside from a handful of skirmishes and soldiers defecting from both sides.

In spite of all the weaponry and bad history, the DMZ is a popular tourist site from the South Korean side and is only around a half-hour drive from Seoul. The Joint Security Zone is the closest point where tourists can view North Korea, and there is a gift shop there that sells North Korean goods such as stamps, money and, according to Thrifty Nomads, wine that 'tastes like nail polish remover'.[1] Tour groups within North Korea also visit, although with a lot less frivolity.

In November 1974, South Korea discovered four tunnels dug by North Korea that crossed under the DMZ. North Korea said they were being used for mining; some tunnels had been painted black to back up the ruse and at any rate, no coal or other minerals were discovered. Later in the decade, the US and South Korea discussed building a wall at the DMZ. (There was no talk of making Kim Il-sung pay for such a wall.) Today, the tunnels are tourist attractions.

---

1 Avery, Jen. 'How to Visit North Korea's DMZ Border (Updated 2018).' Thrifty Nomads, 22 May 2018, http://bit.ly/2whD8CZ.

Even after the brief 2018 summit meetings between Kim Jong-un and Moon Jae-in, it's no picnic zone and silence (other than loudspeakers blaring propaganda, music, and weather reports) doesn't mean peaceful. Plus, there's never been an official peace treaty signed – just an armistice. Put simply, the DMZ is 241 km x 4 km long (150 miles x 2.5 miles) of barbed wire, land mines and heavily armed troops; nuclear power is assumed to be in place. South Korea and the US are reported to keep around 700 soldiers stationed in the area; it's not known how many North Korean troops are there. Overall, the US has around 20,000 troops in South Korea, down from 70,000 shortly after the Korean War ended.

And in spite of Donald Trump's complaints about the cost of keeping US troops in South Korea, that nation pays for most of the cost the US incurs for the sixty-five-plus year guard duty, according to *Bloomberg News*.[2] In 2018, Trump cancelled annual joint US–South Korean military exercises prior to meeting Kim Jong-un.

2 Brands, Hal. 'How Many US Troops Are in Korea? Maybe Too Many.' Bloomberg.com, 30 May 2018, https://bloom.bg/2PDK8lQ.

16. NORTH KOREA'S BORDER TOWN IS A POTEMKIN VILLAGE

Just inside the DMZ near the North Korean border lies Kijong-dong, or Peace Village, a place where no one lives. It's more commonly known as 'Propaganda Village'. It was built in 1953 to lure defectors across the DMZ. Aside from a few disgruntled soldiers, it hasn't delivered. It was the site of a gruesome skirmish in 1973 when North Korean troops axed to death two US soldiers who were trimming a tree supposedly planted by Kim Il-sung. The North Koreans thought it was being cut down.

The town has brightly painted buildings and apartment homes, schools, a hospital and even a day-care centre that supposedly serves the people who work on the collective farm that surrounds the city. North Korea insists there are around 200 residents living here, while the South says the only people they have observed in the village are there to sweep the streets to give the impression they live there. There are people working on the nearby farm, but when they head back to the village after a hard day's work, they park the tractors and leave. Maybe they carpool back to their real homes with the sweepers.

One thing that does distinguish Peace Village is its steady supply of electricity, a rarity in North Korea. Observers on the South Korean side believe everything works on automatic timers. They have noticed that only the top windows in tall buildings light up at night, suggesting that the buildings are literally shells without floors or internal walls. Other buildings have painted-on windows.

In the 1980s, Peace Village got into a flagpole competition with its South Korean counterpart Daeseong-dong. First the South Korean government put up a 98.4-metre-high (323 foot) flagpole. Then Peace Village put up a taller flagpole, 160 metres (525 feet), and hoisted a 270 kg (595 lb) flag on it. It remained the world's tallest flagpole until 2010, when other nations – Azerbaijan, Tajikistan, and Saudi Arabia – built taller ones. You can come to your own conclusions about that.

When it became apparent that South Koreans weren't flocking to Peace Village, the North Korean government began blaring propaganda from loudspeakers. When that didn't bring in the hoped-for refugees, it launched twenty-hour-long daily broadcasts of anti-Western rhetoric, Communist marching band music, and Revolutionary operas. South Korea responded with K-pop music, weather forecasts and news about defections. It must have been quite a racket at the DMZ. You have to wonder if this qualified soldiers guarding the DMZ for hardship pay and how the residents of Daeseong-dong got any sleep. No doubt the sweepers in Peace Village were happy to go home at night, too. Both sides agreed to stop the propaganda broadcasts in 2004.

In February 2018, the noise on the North Korean side was turned down (but not off) and classical music was piped out. The occasion was the opening ceremony of the Olympic Games in Pyeongchang, South Korea, where the North was featured front and centre.

17. NORTH KOREA'S ARMY IS ONE OF THE LARGEST IN THE WORLD

The Global Firepower Index, which ranks 136 countries for its military strength (or GFP) rates North Korea's military as the eighteenth most powerful in the world.[1] The index looks at around fifty items including armed forces and equipment, logistics, and finances.

The Index estimates that around 10 million North Koreans are fit for service. From this number, there are 945,000 active duty personnel and 5.5 million reservists. And in spite of an external debt of $5 trillion ($3.75 trillion), the nation spends $7.5 trillion ($5.68 trillion) on the military.

Here is a summary of the country's conventional military capabilities:

944 aircraft, including 516 bombers, 458 fighters, and 20 attack helicopters

9,935 armoured vehicles; 5,243 combat tanks; and 5,000 rocket projectors

967 naval assets including 438 patrol craft, 86 submarines, 25 mine warfare vessels, and 10 frigates

Both men and women are required to serve in the Korean military. Male high school graduates who are not assigned to go on to college are expected to serve for ten years. Those who go into the workforce must enter the service by age twenty. Until 2003, most men were required to serve for thirteen years. Those in special units still serve thirteen years. In 2015, the country announced that female high school graduates would be required to enlist by age twenty and serve until aged twenty-three.

1 '2018 North Korea Military Strength', *GlobalFirepower.com– World Military Strengths Detailed*, 2018, http://bit.ly/2PCXdf4.

18. North Korea May Have as Many as Sixty Nuclear Bombs

How many nuclear bombs does North Korea have? That's what we call the million-dollar question (£768,500) in the US.

US intelligence believes the country has thirty to sixty nuclear weapons. The Council on Foreign Relations says its arsenal includes short-, medium-, and intermediate-range ballistic missiles; submarine launch capability, and intercontinental ballistic missiles (ICBMs), including one that can be launched via satellite.

In 2017, North Korea successfully tested ICBMs that carry large nuclear warheads. The one it sent over Japan in November reached an altitude of 4,475 km (2,780 miles), higher than the International Space Station and flew around 1,000 km (590 miles) before landing in the Sea of Japan. It was significantly larger and far more powerful than the one it tested just a few months earlier in July.

In 2003, Kim Jong-il withdrew from the Nuclear Non-proliferation Treaty. North Korea first tested a nuclear device – a plutonium-filled atomic bomb – three years later, in October 2006. While this was already older technology, it still was the equivalent of two kilotons of TNT. Another bomb was tested in May 2009. After his father's death, Kim Jong-un sped up nuclear research and the country has detonated weapons four times since he took office: in February 2013, January and September 2016, and September 2017. Each test yielded more kilotons; the one in September 2016 had 35, larger than the nuclear bombs the US dropped on Japan in 1945. The last bomb tested in September 2017 may have been as large as 100 kilotons. That blast may have caused some of the tunnels at Punggye-ri, where North Korea tested underground explosions, to collapse.

It was once believed that North Korea's missiles had faulty guidance systems based on early ones it got from the Soviet Union. But recent military defectors say it now uses GPS technology similar to China's, which is probably quite accurate. China also helped it develop and produce ballistic missiles in the 1970s, and the Soviet Union assisted in building a nuclear research reactor, provided nuclear fuel, and helped it develop other reactor technologies until the 1980s. In the 1990s, the Pakistani scientist Abdul Qadeer Khan provided it with centrifuge technology and designs for a uranium warhead he probably got from China.

North Korea hasn't ignored other weapons research. The Council on Foreign Relations reports it has chemical and biological weapons and may be stockpiling as much as 50,000 tons of chemical weapons, including nerve agents and choking agents. China and the Soviet Union helped it develop these capabilities. Its biological weapons are thought to include anthrax and smallpox; it's unclear if these can be delivered in combat.

The country's conventional military capabilities include 1.1 million people drafted into the army, navy, or air force. It also operates a cyber force that attacks military, political, and civilian targets including banks and at least one Hollywood studio. More information about this cyber army is in Fact 30.

19. The Influence of Confucianism Helps Keep North Korea's Dictatorship Intact

How have North Korea's dictators remained in place for three generations? One popular theory is the role of Confucianism in Korean history.

Confucianism is a blend of philosophy, ideology, and ethics that emerged in China in the sixth and fifth centuries BCE. Its founder, Confucius (551–479 BCE), also known as Kong Qui, came of age during a time when China was ruled by various warlords that left the society in a state of constant flux. Confucius wanted to restore social order and traditional Chinese values such as compassion (not exactly a warlord's biggest concern) by teaching self-discipline and helping guide people into harmonious lives.

The Confucian Golden Rule – 'what you do not wish for yourself, do not do to others' – is probably his most influential contribution. It's also where his beliefs morphed most dramatically outside China.

Like many good ideas, Confucianism can be used for very specific, selfish goals, such as forced obedience from the local population. Korean kings used such neo-Confucian philosophies introduced by later thinkers. By the mid-1500s, Korean society was defined by a rigid set of paternalistic rules for virtually all relationships: fathers and sons, husbands and wives, kings and ministers, and so on. Kim Il-sung added a hefty dose of neo-Confucian thought as he created his personality cult.

Nicholas Levi of the Polish Academy of Sciences argues that Kim Il-sung blended the experiences of the Japanese occupation, the Korean War, and the persistent aim to unify the Korean Peninsula into an ideology that placed the new regime at the head of a united Korean family. It's a fascinating look into the 'Family-State' approach used by kings to promote patriotism that is now used to define the world's only successful hereditary dictatorship.[1]

In the 1960s, the Workers' Party described Kim Il-sung as a god, 'the Sun of Love' who is even mightier than Jesus, Buddha, and Muhammad. Like the historic Buddha, the Kims have come to be seen as spiritual and material leaders for the North Korean nation.

Confucianism is also used to rank people for social and other purposes in South Korea. Writing for the Berkley Center at Georgetown University, Caroline Yarber recalls that during her year studying in South Korea, she noticed that people often ask new acquaintances their age to determine the proper social relationship.

Yarber wrote that the youngest member of her student group was given the most menial job – passing out utensils and pouring drinks at meals. And while some other younger students stepped in to give him a break, older ones never did so. This social pecking order, Yarber notes, also contributes to 'pervasive sexism' (males are inevitably ranked over females) and contributes to dangerous social drinking situations at many workplaces.[2]

1 Levi, Nicholas. 'The Importance of Confucian Values to Kim Jong-il's System.' *Sino-NK*, 28 Aug. 2012, http://bit.ly/2MwxuHj.
2 Yarber, Caroline. 'Confucian Hierarchy in Modern Day Korea.' Georgetown University, 3 Mar. 2015, http://bit.ly/2PH7fMo.

20. NORTH KOREA IS A JUCHE MACHINE

Kim Il-sung created his own special blend of neo-Confucian ideology: Juche. According to North Korea's official website, Juche means 'the masters of the revolution and construction are the masters of the people and that they are also the motive force of the revolution and construction'.[1] Juche's purpose is to venerate Kim and, later, his heirs. The Juche calendar discussed in Fact 28 begins in 1912, the year Kim Il-sung was born. To paraphrase John Lennon, are the Kims more popular than Jesus?

Images of the first two Kims are everywhere in North Korea. There are statues, portraits, and quotations attributed to them in just about every public place. Their photos must be properly displayed in every home, classroom, and office. Echoing traditional Korean art, exotic flowers – kimilsungia and kimjongilia – were created in their honour. Children are taught flowery songs that extol 'love for the leader' and pledge to follow 'the young buds of kimjongilia'.

Propaganda in school extends even to math problems ('if your friend kills two American bastards and you kill four, how many dead American bastards are there?'). Virtually all music, stories, and artwork reflect the Kims' lives and teachings. High school students complete an eighty-one-hour course on Kim Jong-un over a three-year period.

Perhaps the most frightening aspect of Juche are self-criticism sessions in which people are expected to reveal their shortcomings and if they leave something out someone else has observed, such as failing to properly iron a uniform, they can be in for a public shaming that rivals a Donald Trump tweet. In her memoir *Stars Between the Sun*

---

1 'Juche Ideology.' *Democratic People's Republic of Korea_Juche Korea*, Korean Friendship Association, Juche 100 (2011), http://bit.ly/2MzTLE7.

and Moon, North Korean defector Lucia Jang (not her real name) describes keeping a journal of her transgressions – including wearing a wrinkled uniform to school – for the weekly 'saenghwal chonghwa'.[2] Why is this important? Because to fall short of perfection means to dishonour Kim and by extension, the entire nation.

According to the Seoul-based news site *Daily NK*, Kim Jong-un ordered all North Koreans to join a session in his 2016 New Year's address (or if you will, Juche 104). He blamed himself for flood damage in Musan County, which means it's actually the people's responsibility to contain flood damage since he cannot be in the wrong, ever. 'I regretfully confess that I failed [to follow the Marshal's instructions],' a county party leader mourned, and a flood victim testified on the Echo of Unification propaganda site:

> I cried and cried while watching the video of the Marshal [Kim] blaming himself, even though he made us happy by providing new homes before the new year came.[3]

2 Jang, Lucia, and Susan McClelland, *Stars between the Sun and Moon: One Woman's Life in North Korea and Escape to Freedom* (W.W. Norton & Company, 2015).
3 Hwan, Kim Seong, and Bae Min Kwon, 'North Korean Website Reports on Self-Criticism Sessions Following New Year's Address', *Daily NK*, 1 Jan 2017, http://bit.ly/2occTJN.

21. Five US Soldiers Have Defected to North Korea

During the 1960s, four US servicemen stationed in South Korea defected to the North, and another in 1982. No Americans defected during the Korean War.

The 1960s-era defectors were housed together for seven years in a one-room house with no running water. They were taught Juche, studied Kim's writings, and were often beaten by their guards. Later, they were given women, some of whom were kidnapped from other countries, for housekeeping and sex. (Fact 70 discusses North Korea's kidnapping policy.)

The first defector, Larry Alan Abshier, was an army private who abandoned his post and crossed the DMZ in May 1962. According to Charles Jenkins, who defected in 1965, Abshier wasn't particularly bright. The two other defectors they lived with, James Dresnok (defected 1962) and Jerry Wayne Parrish (defected 1963), bullied him and nicknamed him 'Lennie' after the character with an intellectual disability in John Steinbeck's novel *Of Mice and Men*.[1]

Why did they defect? Abshier's reasons aren't known but it's a safe bet that he was bullied in the barracks. Dresnok was an angry man reeling from his wife's infidelity and had recently been convicted of forging leave passes and going AWOL. One day, he simply got up from lunch and raced across the DMZ. Parrish apparently had family problems, while Jenkins hoped his defection would get him sent to the Soviet Union.

All four men got jobs teaching English and translating Kim's works. They also acted in North Korean films. All married and had children. Abshier, Parrish, and Dresnok

---

1 Jenkins, Charles Robert, and Jim Frederick, *The Reluctant Communist: My Desertion, Court-Martial, and Forty-Year Imprisonment in North Korea* (University of California Press, 2008).

lived the rest of their lives in North Korea. Abshier died from a heart attack at age forty and Parrish, who was probably an alcoholic, died from kidney disease at fifty-four. Dresnok's 2016 death was announced in 2017; he was thought to be seventy-five years old.

Jenkins married a Japanese woman who had been kidnapped by North Korean agents. She was eventually reunited with her family and he was permitted to travel to Japan in 2004 for medical treatment. He voluntarily surrendered to the US Army at Camp Zima and pleaded guilty to charges of desertion and aiding the enemy. He served thirty days in the brig, received a dishonourable discharge, and was reduced to the lowest private rank. He died in Japan at age seventy-seven in December 2017.

The last defection came in 1982, by Private Joseph T. White. He shot the lock off a gate leading to the DMZ and was seen walking across it with a duffle bag filled with documents. He recorded a video denouncing the US presence in South Korea. His parents were told on 5 November 1985 – his twenty-fifth birthday – that he had drowned in a river in August and the body was not found. The North Korean government says he was paralysed during an epileptic seizure.

22. North Koreans Speak a Purer and More Violent Form of the Korean Language

The Korean language is spoken throughout the peninsula but like any language it has dialects. While the North-South divide is purely artificial, Korean spoken in the North is a purer form than in the South, says Paul Barby in the North Korea video from his YouTube series *Geography Now!* For one thing, North Korea's isolation from much of the world has limited new vocabulary. Korean spoken in the South has Chinese and English influences. For example, the word for 'juice' in South Korea is 'jyu-seu' while in North Korea it's 'gwa-il dan-mul', which loosely translates to 'fruit sweet water'.[1]

Ben DuMonde points out that South Koreans actually say 'aiseykeulim' for ice cream and 'seongeullaeseu' for sunglasses – a favourite accessory of Kim Jong-il.[2] North and South Korea even have different names for the language: the spoken language is, not unsurprisingly, choseonmal and the written form is choseongul in the North. In the South, it's hangug-eo and hanguel.

Each country also has its own dialects influenced by regions or cities. The dialect spoken in the capital Pyongyang and in the North and South Pyongan provinces is called Pyong'an. People in Hwanghae province speak a completely unique dialect, while people in north-eastern North Korea speak the Yukchin dialect.

People from the North and South can understand one another, although there are linguistic differences in the way some vowels and consonants are pronounced. Problems arise for North Korean defectors when they encounter new words that have entered the South Korean lexicon since

---

1 *Geography Now! North Korea (DPRK)*, Hosted by Paul Barby, 13 December 2017, http://bit.ly/2wqpb5c.

2 DuMonde, B., *Linguistic Differences Between North and South Korean*, 25 October 2017, http://bit.ly/2MCBV3G.

the war. Part of their acclimation includes learning new words about items and concepts they've never heard of. In her memoir *In Order to Live*, North Korean defector and human rights activist Yeonmi Park wryly calls the South Korean language 'Konglish'.[3]

Many people have observed the violent nature of North Korean speech and writing. During her time teaching at Pyongyang University of Science and Technology, Suki Kim noticed a lot of curse words in newspapers, official Workers' Party speeches, poems, and songs. She once watched a dance recital to a song called 'The Song of the Assassin' about hunting down American 'noms' or 'bastards'.[4] As mentioned in Fact 20, schoolchildren are given math problems to determine how many 'Yankee bastards' can be killed ('bastard' seems to be a favourite word) using one or another formula. And yet, one of the photographs in Wendy Simmons' book *My Holiday in North Korea* shows a schoolgirl wearing an Angry Birds cap and a young boy sporting a Mickey Mouse backpack.

3   Park, Yeonmi, and Maryanne Vollers, *In Order to Live: A North Korean Girls Journey to Freedom* (Penguin Press, 2015), p. 214.
4   Kim, Suki, *Without You, There Is No Us: My Time with the Sons of North Korea's Elite* (Crown Publishers, 2014), p. 149.

23. Everyone in North Korea Belongs to an Inminban That Focuses on Cleaning, Spying and Self-criticism

North Korean citizens are banded into inminbans, or People's Groups, which are a key part of the Juche national self-reliance ideology. People are assigned to one based on where they live. Everyone over the age of eight is expected to attend and participate in the local inminban. A version of inminban, the saenghwal chonghwa, operates in schools and universities.

Inminban serve two roles: they ensure everyone pitches in to keep their local areas clean, and they are excellent local spying networks. Heading one is a big responsibility, and most are led by women who have proven their devotion to the Supreme Leader and the Workers' Party. They organise people into different crews to take care of their shared spaces, such as parks, flat hallways and stairwells, gardens, and so on. Some remove rubbish, while others are charged with collecting, tallying, and delivering 'night soil' collections (see Fact 94 for an explanation). The work is done in the mornings. The idea is to enforce people to work together and keep the revolutionary spirit alive no matter how unpleasant the task. Wealthier families in higher songbuns hire others to take care of their inminban duties.

Inminbans are part of North Korea's extensive internal spying network and work closely with the police. Inminban meetings are held once a week to receive reports from individuals about what they've done over the past week and their plans for the immediate future. Weekly inminban ideology meetings include intensive study and review of the Kims' teachings and the infamous self-criticism sessions. Individuals pledge to better themselves on behalf of Kim Jong-un and to honour Kim Il-sung's legacy. If a member fails to report a shortcoming, such as failing to dress properly or bow low enough to a photo of Kim Il-sung, someone will single that person out for exceptionally harsh words, all in public.

Inminban heads are expected to regularly visit and inspect families' private dwellings. They are usually random and can be in the middle of the night. Police may be involved if there is suspicion that a person or family is hoarding food or supplies, hiding illegal literature or videos, or is hosting someone illegally, since internal travel is restricted and requires a permit. Televisions and radios are checked to ensure they are properly sealed and can't be tuned to an illegal (i.e., Chinese or South Korean) station. It's equally important to ensure that the two portraits or photos of the Kims are properly displayed and cleaned.

In recent years, the appeal of heading an inminban has been diminished, Andrei Lankov wrote in *NK News*.[1] They aren't rewarded for their work as in the pre-famine days and in a post-famine world where making money on the side is almost accepted as normal, their intrusions wouldn't go over well with most of the neighbours.

1   Lankov, Andrei. 'The Evolution of North Korea's "Inminban".' *NK News – North Korea News*, 29 May 2018, http://bit.ly/2wrFTkE.

24. North Koreans Are Ranked in Fifty-one Social Categories

The Workers' Paradise, Andrei Lankov observes, enforces the songbun, an unequal system where people inherit their status.[1] It's essentially a caste system.

Kongdan Oh, a senior Asia specialist at the Institute for Defense Analyses, says North Korea relies on a classification system with more than fifty rankings and subgroups that indicate a person's rank:

> A loyal core class, about 25 per cent of the population, which includes working families, descendants of revolutionaries, and descendants of North Korean civilians killed in the Korean War.
>
> About half the population are in the suspect 'wavering' class and include those descended from untrustworthy groups like large landowners and employees of Japanese companies. People suspected of being Christian are usually put in this category.
>
> The remaining 25 per cent come from an unreliable 'hostile' class such as families descended from wealthy, pre-Communist leaders and those who have a member who fled to South Korea.[2]

This system was first launched in 1958 after Kim Il-sung finished purging counter-revolutionaries. He 'unmasked' 100,000 people and executed 2,500, some in public to hold up as an example. Then he ordered an elaborate project to classify the rest, putting each person through eight background checks and conducting loyalty surveys.

---

1 Lankov, Andrei. *North of the DMZ: Essays on Daily Life in North Korea* (McFarland & Company, Inc., 2007), pp. 66–67.

2 Oh, Kongdan, 'Political Classification and Social Structure in North Korea', Brookings, 28 July 2016, https://brook.gs/2BRuVe8.

Seventy thousand people were displaced when it was decreed that people in the 'hostile' class could not live near an international border, within 50 kilometres of Pyongyang or Kaesong, or within 20 kilometres of any city.

Family histories can have devastating consequences since the songbun decides whether a person can go to university and to which one. It determines who gets to live in a city and who stays in the underdeveloped countryside. It determines job assignments and standards of living. In one way, it preserves the social order: parents will not allow their children to marry too far outside their songbun. As Lankov notes, it's not too far off from a feudal system.[3] But it is possible to move up a songbun or two. For example, an exemplary soldier can cancel out a grandparent who embraced a Western religion.

The Kim family sits over everybody else, followed by high-ranking government, military, and security officials. Below them are the People of the Paektu Mountain, descended from Kim Il-sung's guerrilla fighters, and the People of the Naktong River, descendants of high-ranking Korean War military leaders.

One family member can bring down the rest. When Yeonmi Park's uncle was imprisoned, her father and grandfather lost their jobs and the family's relatively high songbun ranking was reduced. Her uncle was released after twelve years because of poor health, a common practice, Park says, that saves the government the cost of paying to have prisoners' remains sent home.[4]

3 Lankov, p. 69.
4 Park and Maryanne Vollers, *In Order to Live*, pp. 25–26.

25. North Korea's Economy Was Killed by Ideology

It's hard to believe that at one time North Korea's economy was one of the strongest in Southeast Asia. The Soviet Union and China invested heavily to rebuild their shared client state and by the 1970s, North Korea's output far outpaced that of South Korea.

So what happened? In a word: ideology.

Rather than follow advice from Moscow about balancing different economic sectors, Kim Il-sung focused far too much on heavy industry. He moved rural populations away from farming; in a country with little arable land, this was disastrous. To make it worse, Kim refused to undermine the Juche ideology discussed in Fact 20 that revolutionary zeal would make up for any shortcomings. After the Soviets reduced their aid, he created something called the Chollima movement, which assured the people that their superhuman efforts would pull the country through anything.

Rather than innovate and plan better, the North Korean government instead put people to work for longer periods to build new projects. Enormous power plants rose up but there was not enough coal to power them. Modern extraction methods would have helped but the country continued to use older, less efficient (and more dangerous) blasting equipment.

Kim even rejected the suggestion to burn oil to generate power because it would mean importing oil and undermining Juche. It's as if he thought that declaring something would happen would make it so. For example, a Six-Year Plan for 1961–1967 proclaimed better living conditions for the people and healthier diets from a renewed focus on agriculture. But resources were diverted, even from heavy industry, to build up the military as the Cold War persisted. Virtually every person from their mid-teens to their early forties was put to work to build underground tunnels for military use.

If importing materials (and food to prevent starvation) was banned, apparently borrowing money was ok. According to Victor Cha, a North Korean specialist for former US President George H. W. Bush, Pyongyang borrowed from the United Kingdom, France, Japan, China, and a few Eastern Bloc nations to buy equipment for planned fertilizer and cement factories. When Czechoslovakia asked for its debt to be repaid, Kim 'negotiated' payment with a 200-year supply of ginseng root, reputed to boost sexuality. The country defaulted on almost all its loans.[1]

Even today, the North Korean economy is stagnant in spite of having a lot of mineral wealth. *Business Insider* reported in 2017 that it has some of the largest deposits in the world of gold, iron, copper, zinc, magnetite, limestone, tungsten, and graphite. The total value might be as high as *$10 trillion*![2] But it can't be used because the country doesn't have the infrastructure to export anything on a large scale.

1 Cha, Victor D., *The Impossible State North Korea, Past and Future* (Harper Collins, 2013), p. 117.
2 Weller, Chris, 'North Korea Is Sitting on a Stockpile of Minerals Worth Trillions', *Business Insider*, 29 June 2017, https://read.bi/2PdMwPp.

26. North Koreans Are Required to Wear Loyalty Badges Portraying the First Two Kims

'In the late 1970s,' Andrei Lankov writes in his set of essays *North of the DMZ*, 'North Korean students could occasionally be seen on the streets on my native Leningrad,' distinguished from Chinese and Vietnamese students by their ubiquitous Kim badges.[1]

To this day, all North Koreans, even Kim Jong-un, wear loyalty badges to show their devotion to the nation's founder. There are around twenty types of badges that are given to establish a person's place within the songbun. Not surprisingly, the size of a badge matters in displaying one's credentials and rank. People in the lower ranks of the songbun wear small round badges, but youth who are active in the Socialist League wear larger round ones. Military cadets wear badges with Kim Jong-il's image. Badges are never worn on overcoats.

The rarest badges, Lankov says, feature the first two Kims against the background of a red banner. It's actually a reissue from badges released in the early 1980s; Kim Jong-il was supposedly reluctant to be elevated to his father's status.

At first, only Party leaders wore badges but they were soon required for everyone. Early badges showed a rather stern-looking Kim Il-sung; later ones released after his death featured his smiling image. A Kim Jong-il badge was released following his death. It was reported in 2015 that Kim Jong-un presented 3,000 special badges with his image to top officials and youth party leaders.

Not even during the 'crazy days of Mao's cult',[1] Lankov writes, were his subjects required to wear his image. But in the early 1970s, someone in the North Korean government

---

1 Lankov, *North of the DMZ: Essays on Daily Life in North Korea*, p.7.

hit on the idea that true believers should wear the Great Leader's image on their person at all times. There was a mass production of badges with Kim's official portrait. By Kim Il-sung's sixtieth birthday in 1972, every adult wore one. To this day, people are expected to wear their Kim badge(s) whenever they appear in public. Failing to wear a badge will be noted and discussed at the next inminban session!

There are special badges for special occupations. The Sonyondan, or Children's Union, presents badges bearing the likenesses of Kim Il-sung and Kim Jong-il to children when they turn twelve. Sonyondan was created in the image of the old Soviet Young Pioneers, which in turn was inspired by the Boy Scouts and should not be confused with the Bangtan Sonyondan, or Bangtan Boys, a South Korean boy band whose first album, *2 Cool 4 Skool*, launched them into K-pop stardom.

The badges are designed and manufactured by the Mansudae Art Studio (formerly Mansudae Creative Group), which employs 4,000 people, including around 800 artists according to its website (https://www.mansudaeartstudio.com). The artwork on the website is owned by an Italian company and was purchased before the UN sanctions went into effect. It does not, however, sell badges.

27. THERE'S A COLLECTORS' MARKET FOR NORTH KOREAN LOYALTY BADGES

Surely you aren't shocked to read that there is a collectors' market for loyalty badges!

In 2016, Reuters discovered Thomas Hui, a Hong Kong resident who may have the largest collection of loyalty badges outside North Korea. He first visited Pyongyang in 2008 and was fascinated by the badges. At the time, he couldn't obtain any, but over the years amassed more than 100 badges he believes were smuggled out of North Korea by Chinese workers.[1]

AvaxNews sent a photographer to snap Hui's collection; check it out at http://bit.ly/2MA2Gpm.

Foreigners can buy their own badges with a 100 euro donation to the Kim Il-sung & Kim Jong-il Foundation (http://naenara.com.kp/en/). You don't even have to join the foundation. That said, I couldn't find a purchase link.

The double-Kim badges appear to be the most valued by collectors, if eBay is anything to go by. As Radio Free Asia reported a few years ago, 'two Kims are better than one'. At the time, a black market had sprung up for them in North Korea, partly in reaction to a 2013 crackdown on the quasi-illegal methamphetamine market. Because they sell relatively well or can be exchanged for goods or services, badge dealers there referred to the double Kims as their nest eggs.[2]

---

1 'Former Hong Kong Bank Worker Amasses North Korean Badge Collection', Reuters, Thomson Reuters, 12 Apr 2016, https://reut.rs/2BRv5Cg.

2 'Illegal Sale of "Double Portrait" Lapel Pins Flourishes in North Korea', Radio Free Asia, 30 Jan 2015, http://bit.ly/2LpSo5G.

28. North Korea Keeps Its Own Calendar but Changed Its Time Zone to Match the South's

In 1997, Kim Jong-il created a new Juche calendar for North Korea that begins in 1912, the year of Kim Il-sung's birth, known as Juche 1. It was formally implemented on 9 September, the Day of the Foundation of the Republic.

The calendar combines a traditional Korean calendar with the modern Gregorian one. Kim Il-sung's birthday, 15 April, is a national holiday called Day of the Sun. Other holidays mark the start and finish of the Gregorian calendar such as Chosongul Day that commemorates the adoption of the Korean alphabet in 1443; the Korean New Year; and several other traditional Korean holidays like Buddha's birthday (Chopail) and major events in modern North Korean history.

Back in August 2015, North Korea set back its clocks a half-hour to create a new time zone: Pyongyang Time. The move was due to the untenable situation of being in the same time zone as Japan, still an arch-enemy for its occupation of the peninsula during the early part of the twentieth century. But after Kim Jong-un visited South Korea's President Moon Jae-in in 2018, the country pushed its clocks forward to match South Korea's time zone. North Korea's official news service reported that Kim Jong-un found it 'painful' to see two different clocks in the summit house. Syncing with South Korea is 'the first practical step for national reconciliation and unity'.[1]

---

1 'DPRK resets Pyongyang time to align with S. Korea.' *Xinhuanews*, 30 April 2018, http://bit.ly/2NjcGQ1.

29. NORTH KOREA IS A MAJOR DEALER IN BANNED AND COUNTERFEIT DRUGS

North Korea has performed exceptionally well manufacturing and distributing illegal drugs – especially heroin, cocaine, and high-grade methamphetamine – throughout Southeast Asia. It also manufactures and sells counterfeit drugs, primarily Viagra, Cialis, and fentanyl, a powerful opioid used in painkillers. Since the rate of cigarette smoking is very high in the region, it also makes counterfeit cigarettes.

It distributes the drugs and cigarettes through its network of embassies throughout Southeast Asia, taking advantage of diplomatic immunity from searches and seizures. For this reason, the country is called, quite rightly, 'Narco Korea'.

Much of this activity supports the nation's nuclear endeavours and is directed by top members of its military and diplomatic corps who work through a group called 'Central Committee Bureau 39'.

For several years, North Korea was a major provider of crystal methamphetamine, which was widely used there as a painkiller and stimulant until a crackdown began in 2013. One drugs researcher in Seoul told UPI in 2016 that at least 30 per cent of North Koreans regularly use meth and opium.[1] Under Kim Jong-un, the focus has been on Amidon, a poppy-derived opioid similar to morphine. Hamhung, the country's second-largest city, has become the hub for Amidon production.

Other illegal pursuits include trafficking banned products such as rhino horns and ivory, 'conflict' diamonds, and currency counterfeiting, for which it did such a good job that the US redesigned much of its paper money.

---

1 Shim, Elizabeth. 'More than 30 Percent of North Koreans Use Meth, Opium.' UPI, 1 Dec. 2016, http://bit.ly/2Lv60wn.

30. THE NORTH KOREAN GOVERNMENT IS A REAL GANGSTA'S PARADISE

When it comes to gangsta, the guy Coolio sang about in 1995 has nothing on Kim Jong-un. North Korea is his very own gangsta's paradise.

An entity called Room 39, which is discussed in Fact 32, directs illegal activities on behalf of the government, including manufacturing and distributing counterfeit drugs (Viagra is popular) and illicit ones such as methamphetamine. It also created fake US $100 bills, which prompted an overhaul of US currency production.

In the face of UN sanctions and tougher ones from the US and its allies, North Korea is said to be considering getting back into the meth game and restarting 'bingdu' production, which is described as a 'high-quality, chemically pure' substance that was 'professionally packaged and shipped' to the Philippines, Japan, and Australia, according to Sheena Greitens, a professor at the University of Missouri who directs its Institute for Korean Studies.[1] The trade is worth billions of dollars, says Italian journalist Loretta Napoleoni, and can be secretly conducted using crypto currencies, making it nearly impossible to trace a money path. Myanmar is currently the biggest producer; with state backing, North Korea can quickly and easily outpace it.[2]

North Korea doesn't have a lot of influence in Africa like China does, but it's been an open secret for decades that it's been involved in smuggling ivory and rhino horn from its embassies. In 1989, Zimbabwe's Environmental

---

1 Hamilton, Keegan. 'North Korean Meth, Motorcycle Gangs, Army Snipers, and a Guy Named Rambo.' *VICE News*, 18 Mar. 2014, http://bit.ly/2BRhhaY.
2 Napoleoni, Loretta *North Korea: the Country We Love to Hate* (UWA Publishing, 2018).

Investigation Agency noted that the North Korean embassy was 'deeply involved in the illegal ivory and rhino horn trade', reports the Global Initiative Against Transnational Organized Crime. Three years later, the country expelled a young diplomat for smuggling rhino horns. Today, that diplomat, Han Tae-song, is North Korea's representative to the United Nations.[3]

In 2017, the Global Initiative further linked North Korea's embassies in Africa to tobacco and mineral rackets as well. One defector who ran a North Korean front company from Beijing told the group that diplomats returned from Africa with contraband two or three times a year, a serious abuse of diplomatic immunity to say the least. Sanctions, the initiative concludes, will further expand such activity.

For a while, North Korea spent a lot of time teaching students to pirate video games and ironically, security software. Many were employed by a Chinese firm operating from Pyongyang. Since then, the regime has ramped up its hacking capers. In 2017, it released the WannaCry ransomware that took advantage of old Microsoft Windows users. In 2015, it infiltrated emails used at Sony Pictures to expose some embarrassing opinions, apparently in retaliation for the upcoming release of the Seth Rogan satire *The Interview*. Chaos may well be North Korea's power play.

---

3 *Diplomats and Deceit: North Korea's Criminal Activities in Africa*, http://bit.ly/2Lt4Pxm.

31. ROOM 39 IS BOTH OFFICIAL AND ILLICIT

North Korea's government-run gang operations are known as Room 39. Its official title is Central Committee Bureau 39 of the Workers' Party of Korea. It's also called Bureau, Division, or Office 39, which should not be confused with a future Microsoft product. Its official purpose is to provide slush funds, usually in foreign currency, for the Kims' enjoyment.

Kim Il-sung launched Room 39 in the late 1970s. Kim Jong-il was reported to have started a similar operation called Room 38 to handle legal business deals for the family. South Korean media later reported it merged with Room 39. A high-ranking Central Committee official and former Kim Jong-il classmate runs Room 39. You have to wonder if he's making plans for an eventual escape given the fate of many old Kim family comrades.

The Australian Broadcast Corporation interviewed a high-ranking Room 39 defector in January 2018 who confirmed it continues to focus on raising foreign currency for the 'Revolutionary Fund' account for Kim Jong-un, who takes in around 40 per cent of the economy for himself and top leaders. The defector is a former agent for the Daesong Group, the parent company of around 300 companies that serves as Room 39's official face and controls most of North Korea's foreign trade. (It should not be confused with Daesung Group, a South Korean company that works with renewable energy.) He was involved in selling ginseng and gemstones, and oversaw gold smuggling into China where it was sold on the international market as Chinese gold. China made it 'easy', he said, to bypass UN sanctions. 'You just change company names and have branches in other countries.'[1]

---

1 Carney, Matthew. 'Inside North Korea's Shadowy Office 39: Defector Reveals How Kim Jong-un Gets His Cash.' *ABC News*, Australian Broadcasting Corporation, 6 Jan. 2018, https://ab.co/2MqbduX.

Daesong Group owns a bank, Daesong Bank, in Pyongyang. North Korea expert Andrei Lankov says Daesong Bank's work is largely in legitimate trade, dominated by seafood exports and sales of gold, iron, coal, and labour. It has some involvement in illegal trade and often props up sham corporations whose sole purpose is to get hard currency for the regime. It reportedly is not tasked with funding North Korea's nuclear ambitions.[2]

In 2014, a senior bank official, Yun Tae-hyong, disappeared during a business trip in Russia with around $5 million (£3.8 million). It was apparently a defection, something of a surprise given Russia's reluctance to accept North Korean defectors, as discussed in Fact 69. I was unable to find any reports on Yun since his disappearance, which also occurred less than a year after Kim Jong-un arrested and killed his own uncle for treason.

Room 39's earliest work included creating high-quality counterfeit US $50 and $100 'super notes' and pushing $15 million to $25 million into circulation each year until around 2011. There are reports that it's restarted this effort in response to UN- and US-led sanctions.

2 Lankov, Andrei. 'The Shadowy World of North Korea's Palace Economy.' *Al Jazeera*, 3 Sept. 2014, http://bit.ly/2MC1eSv.

32. North Korean Gangs Focus on Smuggling

In North Korea, true gang activity is conducted by the government, as discussed in Fact 31. Gangs smuggle goods in and out of the country and are hired by defectors to lead them out. Many of these activities take place along the Chinese border in the northern part of the country where it's relatively easy to cross a couple of rivers, as defectors have done for decades. Gangs interact with Chinese triads, but aren't nearly as organised and wealthy; they work more like networks than anything else.

The father of the defector and human rights activist Yeonmi Park supplemented his income through smuggling. Living near the Yalu River, it was easy to enter the local black market, which Park describes as providing 'everything from dried fish to electronics', imported from China.[1] He started by reselling Chinese cigarettes in the North Korean interior, using medical notes to authorise his travel.

Park's father took an official job with less supervision and began moving more luxurious commodities such as Chinese clothing and toiletries. Growing up, the family lived a relatively privileged life with enough food, meat a few times a month (rare for people outside the higher songbun), and luxuries such as toothpaste, shampoo, and medicine – items her father also sold. The family continued to live like most rural people, in a small home without electricity or a steady supply of running water. One plus: it was conveniently located next to a train station!

When money got tight, or there were crackdowns on smuggling, Park's parents went to a private lender. That got a bit more dangerous than Park's mother was comfortable with – they were, after all, loan sharks – and her father

---

1 Park and Vollers, *In Order to Live*, p. 27.

decided to begin selling valuable metals to the Chinese. That put him in contact with wealthier Pyongyang networks and became lucrative enough that he could bribe officials, who themselves needed money to feed their families, so he could travel at will. He stayed in comfortable apartments and even took his daughters to see Pyongyang. The family was largely spared from the worst of the 1990s famine; Park writes about seeing 'kochebi' street children at train stations eating rotting food and wondering how they survived.

Things went pretty well until Park's father acquired a girlfriend, something not terribly uncommon among 'wealthy' North Koreans. That seemed to trigger his downfall. Gang members will inform on one another for profit or safety, and one informer turned the girlfriend in to the police. Park's father was picked up as he approached her home, which was being watched because someone had informed on him as well.

Later, after being smuggled out of North Korea with her mother, the thirteen-year-old Park ended up working for their smuggler, a major figure in the local gang scene. She quickly learned Chinese and was put to work to use her bilingual skills to take recent arrivals to their new 'homes'.

33. NORTH KOREA HAS LIMITED INTERNET

What passes for the internet for most North Koreans is called the Kwangmyong, an intranet connection run by China Unicom since 2010. It has around 170 websites. Access to the open, global network is prohibited to all but the most elite. But China Unicom does a pretty good job given the limited resources it has to work with. In Pyongyang, at least, there's videoconferencing from factories to headquarters, and online lectures from Kim Il-sung University.

In 2017, a state-owned Russian telecomm firm, TransTeleCom, gave the country an actual internet connection. It certainly gives the country far more opportunity for cyber attacks as well as protecting its infrastructure. In fact, the US Cyber Command shut down North Korean hackers literally hours before the new connection went live by sending a DOS (denial of service) attack. Notably, TransTeleCom belongs to Russian Railways, an enormous state-owned transportation and infrastructure company with deep ties to Vladimir 'Hack? What hack?' Putin.

Those North Koreans who do have access to the actual internet keep safe and mostly visit Chinese sites. According to *Foreign Policy* magazine, they like to play Western online games, PlayStation and Nintendo games, and platforms such as Steam. But analysts have also found them visiting sites such as Kaspersky and Symantec, and engineering departments at top US universities.[1]

North Korea also runs a Bitcoin operation and is mining Monero, a more anonymous crypto currency.

---

1 Groll, Elias. 'North Korean Internet Users Shun Facebook and Google for Chinese Alternatives.' *Foreign Policy*, 25 Apr. 2018, http://bit.ly/2Nlyevc.

34. NORTH KOREA'S FRIEND ZONE IS SHRINKING

To borrow a phrase from one of my favourite YouTube shows, *Geography Now!* (https://www.youtube.com/ GeographyNow), North Korea's 'Friend Zone' is shrinking thanks to its nuclear adventures, human rights violations, and drug trafficking activities. The United Nations Security Council has passed several sanctions against the country since it withdrew from the Nuclear Non-Proliferation Treaty in 2003. The sanctions range from capping energy and weapon imports to North Korea to banning North Korean exports, including labour, and restricting fishing rights. The European Union and United States passed additional sanctions that prevent a lot of business and trade with North Korea.

Five UN members do not recognise North Korea at all and do not have any direct diplomatic exchanges either through an embassy or the United Nations. They are the United States, Japan, France, South Korea, and Israel, which was never recognised by North Korea. And for what it's worth, Taiwan, which is not a UN member, does not recognise Pyongyang either.

Spain, Kuwait, Peru, and Mexico expelled North Korean ambassadors and diplomats from their embassies following North Korea's nuclear test on 3 September 2017. Egypt, the Philippines, and Uganda scaled back trade, training, and military ties as well. The nuclear tests, drug trafficking, and human rights violations have strained a lot of other relations too. Some nations that technically have diplomatic relations with North Korea have little to nothing to do with the country:

Armenia – technically started contact in 1992 after it gained independence from the Soviet Union but never allowed it to progress due to human rights violations

Australia – very strained due to drug trafficking and nuclear violations

Botswana – broke off ties in 2014 over human rights violations

Canada – suspended diplomatic relations in 2010

New Zealand – relies on its Ambassador to South Korea but has nearly no contact.

China remains North Korea's closest ally, although it clearly doesn't have much control over its nuclear ambitions. It provided the country with around 90 per cent of its imports in 2016 – and it voted to support the latest round of sanctions in December 2017.

There is a British embassy in Pyongyang, which sits inside a compound that used to be the East Germany embassy, and serves British nationals living in or visiting North Korea. Sweden represents American, Australian, and Canadian interests in North Korea, as well as Nordic Country interests that fall outside of the EU zone. It shares its embassy with the German, French, and UK missions. France's mission is mainly humanitarian and cultural and includes promoting French in North Korea, supplying teachers to Kim Il-sung University and Pyongyang University of Foreign Languages. Anyway, its interests are represented by the European Union embassy.

North Korea has an embassy in London, although it's outside of it, at 73 Gunnersbury Ave, near the Popefield Playing Fields. Only Cambodia and Eritrea also have embassies outside central London. In 2016, North Korea's Deputy Ambassador, Thae Yong-ho, defected to South Korea with the help of MI6.

35. NORTH KOREA IS GROWING ITS TECHNOLOGY SECTOR

In spite of relying on others for internet access, North Korea is growing its tech sector.

In keeping with Juche ideology, it is trying to do most of this on its own. Its Ullim desktops, based on open-access Linux tools to make it look more like a Mac, are at top universities – donated by the Dear Respected Leader Kim Jong-un – and run Red Star operating systems developed by the government's IT research centre, Korea Computer Center. They access the Kwangmyong intranet through the Naenara ('my country') browser reported to be a modified type of Firefox. Red Star 3.0 has email, a calendar, time zone settings, and a 'kPhoto' feature.

Older computers use outdated Windows XP systems, and they had the same problems in 2017 as the rest of the world when the decommissioned software was exploited by Wanna Decryptor ransomware.

Being the products of a police state, computers are loaded with spyware. Computers smuggled outside the country show that any attempt to disable core functions causes an automatic reboot. Any files downloaded from USBs are watermarked for security purposes. Trace viewers, used in the West for logging and trouble-shooting, take screenshots that can't be deleted or accessed by non-officials.

Most computers are in libraries, universities and offices; according to Reuters, fewer than 20 per cent of households have a computer.[1]

Mobile phones were introduced in North Korea in late 2002. Within one year, 20,000 people owned one. Reuters

---

1 Miles, Tom. 'Tackling North Korea's Chronically Poor Sewage "Not Rocket Science": UN', Reuters, 20 June 2018, https://reut.rs/2MvYOp8.

reports that nearly 70 per cent of North Korean households owned a mobile phone in 2017. They are, however, cut off from the rest of the world. Foreigners use a different mobile network and cannot make or receive domestic calls. They can try to buy a local phone but it will be stripped of apps and features and blocked from adding any.

Shortly after Kim Jong-un came to power, mobile phones got a huge boost to 3G thanks to investment from Egypt's Orascome and Loxley Pacific from Thailand. Otherwise, North Koreans can use their mobile devices to play games, surf the Kwangmyong, take pictures, and get services such as weather forecasts and dictionaries. One of the most popular games, according to the Associated Press, is called 'Boy General'.[2]

While most phones are Android knock-offs, there are also iPhone and iPad imitations: the Jindallae and Ryonghung iPad. WiFi is not available, and since 2014, all mobile phones automatically reject apps or media that don't have, literally, a seal of approval from the government. Ironically, that technology was lifted from Apple itself and was originally used to detect unauthorised use of App Store products.

Kim Jong-un has been shown in front of actual Apple products including a MacBook Pro – the same technology that produced this book.

2 Associated Press. 'North Korea's Internet Is as Weird as You Think It Is.' *Fox News*, 10 Nov. 2017, https://fxn.ws/2od8GFX.

36. Mobile Phones Are Far More Common in North Korea than Landlines

As in most developing nations, mobile phones in Korea far outnumber landlines. Much of this is due to the fact that landlines for the average citizen have never been a priority and are allocated for government officials and government operations. The CIA's World Factbook says there were 1.8 million landlines in North Korea in 2016.[1] Perhaps 10 per cent of them are in private homes.

Paul French wrote in his 2007 book *North Korea: The Paranoid Peninsula* that getting a landline requires completing a form to indicate social rank, why the phone is wanted, and an explanation as to how it will be paid for.[2] It's safe to assume that private landlines are limited to those in higher-ranking Juche categories. Before mobiles hit the scene, ordinary North Koreans made their phone calls from work, a telephone bureau office, at post offices, and at public phones on the streets.

According to *The Epoch Times*, an independent non-profit media service popular in Chinese communities (it was founded by Chinese-American adherents of Falun Gong), North Korea did a major reorganisation of landline assignments in 2017 after it learned an official phone directory of government offices and officials had been smuggled out of the country. The book's contents were classified, and a number of people were arrested along the Chinese border where smuggling is rampant. All this was quite a headache for the small merchant class, who prefer the cheaper landline fees to mobile phone costs.[3]

1 Country Comparison Telephones – Fixed Lines. Central Intelligence Agency, http://bit.ly/2OLvEz3.
2 French, Paul, *North Korea: the Paranoid Peninsula* (Zed Books, 2007), p.22
3 Little, Matthew. 'North Korea Cuts Phones, Hunts Down Phone Books, After Directory Leaked.' 14 Dec. 2017, *The Epoch Times*, http://bit.ly/2PFbpEs.

Luckily for them, mobile phones are pretty common in North Korea these days. Their numbers tripled between 2011 and 2016, the *Nikkei Asian Review* reported in late 2017, bringing the total numbers to 3.61 million, or around one for every seven people.[4]

Most mobile phone owners subscribe to a provider called KoryoLink, which provides 2G and 3G services and is the only service available to visitors, who can purchase a SIM card and use their own phones while they are in the country to make calls outside Korea; they will not be able to place local calls. KoryoLink's 3G base is limited to Pyongyang, but its 2G operates throughout much of the country. Kumsan, the first 2G network, covers the entire country and is used mostly outside Pyongyang where people have older phones. The Rason Special Economic Zone, one of several in the country, has its own 3G network run by a Thai company.

Check out this webpage where you can listen to sample KoryoLink recordings: https://wills.co.tt/bitbucket/koryolink/. It was created by Will Scott, an American who has taught IT in Pyongyang and Cuba and blogs on internet and online access issues.

---

4 Yamada, Kenichi. 'North Korea's Cell Phone Users Triple.' *Nikkei Asian Review*, 15 Dec. 2017, https://s.nikkei.com/2obZIZh.

37. North Korea Has Two, Maybe Three, Car Manufacturers

Not many North Koreans own cars, and not many are manufactured there. But there are at least two car manufacturers: Pyeonghwa Motors, established by the Unification Church in 2000 and handed over to the North Korean government in 2013, and Pyongchang Auto Works, which split from Sungri Motor Plant, a manufacturer of larger motor vehicles.

Pyeonghwa wasn't exactly a screaming success and the Unification Church was probably relieved to be rid of it. Even today, it only produces around 2,000 cars each year. In 2015, it provided a brochure that indicated twenty-five models. They aren't particularly powerful; *Mashable* reports maximum 80 horsepower (hp) compared to a Toyota, which has 178 hp. Some look a bit like Kias and Volkswagens, while others 'seem to have been conceived during a toddler's dream fever', *Mashable* opines.[1] Other models are based on Fiats and China's Shuguang car. In 2015, Pyeonghwas were priced at £7,700–£23,000 ($10,000–$30,000) and were thought to be manufactured in another country and assembled in North Korea. It is the *only* company in North Korea permitted to advertise on billboards and television!

Park Sang-gwon, a former Pyeonghwa president, told a Unification Church website in 2011 that the company employs people from Japan, Vietnam and China, and that he is a US citizen. At the time, the church still owned 70 per cent of the company because North Korea, Park said, didn't have enough money to invest any more. He also claimed the company earned a $1 million (£7.7 million) profit that year.

1 Power, John. 'Yes, North Korea Makes Cars, and Here Are the Latest Models.' *Mashable*, 2 Nov. 2015, http://bit.ly/2Nlv5vF.

After the church pulled out of Pyeonghwa in 2013, it was largely written off. Two years later, though, the church-owned UPI reported that two models, the Whistle, a sedan, and Cuckoo, an SUV, were common sights in Pyongyang. They cost £6,950–£7,700 ($9,000–$10,000) each.[2]

I was unable to find much about Pyongchang Auto Works, which makes a kind of Jeep and a couple of other vehicles including a modified 4x4 pickup truck.

In January 2018, North Korea announced a line of luxury cars from Chongphung, a venture with an unnamed outside company (probably from China), which also happens to violate UN sanctions. There is a Chinese company with the same name, but it's not clear if it's the same entity. Anyway, owning a Chongphung is probably something of a status symbol: the line includes an SUV, a saloon (sedan to us Yanks), and a minibus. They are part of the Naenara line, which means 'my country', and underscores that the patriotic thing to do is to buy one if you can afford it.

And that is the problem. The average salary in North Korea is just £850 per year ($1,100).

2   Shim, Elizabeth. 'North Korea's Pyeonghwa Cars Crowd the Streets of Pyongyang.' UPI, 10 Dec. 2015, http://bit.ly/2PCZAyu.

38. North Korea Has Limited Television Programming

North Korean television programming for the masses is pretty limited. I say this from the US, where network TV is a real yawner except for the Public Broadcasting Service – and half its content comes from the BBC! I skipped through an hour of a North Korean broadcast someone posted on YouTube in 2017, apparently via 4Chan. Here's what I saw:

> Ballets, including one featuring women dancing in Korean Army uniforms, and another about a Christian clergyman who steals and kills a little boy who, I must say, is an excellent dancer
>
> Documentaries about North Korean communications/spying, clothing manufacturing and assembly, science/dinosaurs, and mining
>
> A long announcement I'm sure was meant to stir up patriotic feelings
>
> A music video showing a lot of marching and scenes of busy, focused workers
>
> A children's talent show.

Watch it here: https://youtu.be/jSRjJ7Ss88o.

The documentaries didn't look too bad but if this is the daily menu, I can understand why there's an old joke about an elderly woman in the countryside whose grandson sends her a TV. After a month, she sends it back and asks for another because 'we've finished watching this one'.

Former Pyongyang English instructor Suki Kim wrote that 'when there was electricity', she turned on her TV to combat loneliness. There were four stations in Pyongyang at the time: Choson Central, Korean Educational and Cultural Network (KECN), and Mansudae, a weekend-only station.

She never got to see KECN, which broadcast for just a couple of hours a day. She watched Choson's evening line-up: news with photos (no video) of Kim Jong-il, a karaoke-style music programme complete with lyrics on the screen, a drama or film, and another news broadcast. Sometimes programmes were interrupted with quotes from the Kims. Each night ended with something called *The Report by the Unification and Peace Committee*, a 'soliloquy berating South Korea and the United States, using oddly colloquial expressions like "freaking out" and "cut the crap"'.[1]

South Korean news organisations are permitted to have satellites that pick up North Korean televisions, although private citizens cannot have them. A January 2018 report from an ABC correspondent visiting Seoul said that North Korea's Korean Central TV (KCTV) broadcasts feature two daily news reports and lots of tributes to all the Kims, followed by anti-US propaganda. Then there are reports on factories and collective farms: factories continuously break new records and create the best-quality merchandise anywhere, while the manure collection effort described in Fact 94 has been wildly successful.

Foreign news reporting is summed up with this message: 'foreign countries are horrible places to live' and North Koreans 'should appreciate their ... fortunate lives'.[2]

I don't think the Kims watched much broadcast television. Kim Jong-il had one of the world's largest film libraries and no need for it, and I'll bet his son gets the NBA channel.

---

1 Kim, *Without You There is No Us*, pp. 215-216.
2 Lee, Hakyung Kate. 'What I Learned from Watching a Week of North Korean TV.' *ABC News*, 31 Jan. 2018, https://abcn. ws/2obUU6k.

39. Famine Killed as Many as 3.5 Million North Koreans in the 1990s

North Korea suffered an extreme famine from 1994 to 1998. A lot of unfortunate events converged during those years:

Economic mismanagement caused by inflexible centralised planning

Floods and droughts in different parts of the country which centralised planning wouldn't, or couldn't, overcome

Inability to overcome the loss of Soviet support, which had propped up the Kim regimes.

To make matters worse, only around 20 per cent of North Korea's land can be farmed. Most of the country is dominated by mountains and is covered by frost for at least half the year. When flood or drought hits the few arable areas, the impact is sizable.

The typical North Korean diet has never been nutritious. Food is allocated according to political and songbun standing, so those in the lower songbun never got much to begin with. As an example, the World Food Program considers 600 g of cereal per day to be less than a survival ration. Before the famine, 'privileged industrial workers' were given 900 g a day, and 'ordinary workers' 700 g. Retirees only received 300 g per day! In 1987, these meagre rations were reduced by 10 per cent and again in 1992. Even more reductions followed in 1994 and 1997, when some people were given just 128 g of cereal each day.

Food and energy imports essentially ended when the Soviet Union collapsed for good in December 1991. Then, floods hit North Korea's coal mines – one of the country's few moneymakers – resulting in an additional loss of energy resources. So the mines couldn't produce coal and the miners weren't working and eventually stopped getting paid.

This made it even more difficult for them to trade or buy food on the black market. And since the country's infrastructure ran on coal, electricity became scarce and farms soon ran out of power to run equipment. This created a vicious cycle the country couldn't overcome.

China stepped in to fill the gap left by the former Soviet Union, establishing itself as North Korea's new sponsor. But it couldn't provide enough. As people were literally dropping dead in the streets, the North Korean government finally gave in and turned to the international community for help. One American relief expert told *The New York Times* in June 1997 that farmers were so weak the government sent soldiers, who received better rations, to plant rice for the upcoming season. An official admitted to him that many elderly people stopped eating altogether so their grandchildren could eat.[1]

In an attempt to rally its starving people, the government created a special name for the crisis: the Arduous March, or the March of Suffering. This euphemism was meant to cast blame entirely on outside causes for the famine, rather than admit any wrongdoing on the part of the government led by the infallible Dear Leader.

1 Crossette, Barbara. 'Hunger in North Korea: A Relief Aide's Stark Report.' *The New York Times*, 10 June 1997, https://nyti.ms/2MByXMI.

40. Much of the Food Aid Delivered to North Korea Disappeared

North Korea does not provide statistics on famine-related deaths, but professional observers using data from people allowed to enter the country to help, came up with that number of people who died from starvation or hunger-related sicknesses being as high as 3.5 million.[1] The government gave food priority to Pyongyang – the only face of North Korea that was virtually available to the rest of the world – and the military. Everyone else, including farmers, had their rations cut.

If you've ever spent any time on a farm, you know it's hard work and requires a lot of energy. The fuel shortage meant tractors weren't running on large government-owned farms, so work had to be done manually, just as on smaller farms. As their food allowances shrank, people who worked on small farms became too weak to work, particularly in regions where floods left muddy fields that were difficult to plough by hand. Farmers who could grow anything kept as much as they could for themselves; as Jordan Weissmann reported in *The Atlantic* in 2011, half the corn crop was missing by 1996. Soldiers were sent to guard farms so that they, too, could eat.[2]

North Korea received around $42.4 billion in food aid over a decade. Food aid came from China, as well as South Korea, the European Union, and incredibly, Japan and the United States. Japan actually provided the bulk of the earliest food aid and continued to give generously through

---

1 Noland, Marcus, et al. 'Famine in North Korea: Causes and Cures.' *Economic Development and Cultural Change*, July 2001, pp. 741–767. Working paper at http://bit.ly/2Lt2pPF.

2 Weissmann, Jordan. 'How Kim Jong Il Starved North Korea.' *The Atlantic*, 20 Dec. 2011, http://bit.ly/2PGYe5R.

3 'Food Assistance.' North Korea in the World, http://bit.ly/2wsmoZ9.

2001.[3] However, much of the aid was stolen by the country's elites, who resold it on the black markets. Farmers often did the same with the crops they hoarded.

North Korean defector Lucia Jang writes that as rations were cut and eventually ended, people's personalities changed. Theft became common, and people sold clothing and furniture for food. She became so desperate she traded sex for food.[4]

Barbara Demick, who interviewed famine survivors, wrote about one woman who rose early every morning to scrounge for weeds that sprouted overnight. Hoping these tender 'greens' would be easier to digest, she cooked them with bark and added a little salt and cornmeal to make a porridge.[5] But as Demick notes, people who are starving will die from eating 'substitute foods that their bodies can't digest'. Famine affects the youngest – children under age five – for whom a simple cold or upset tummy quickly becomes fatal. And many of the famine's victims were those who were too young to steal or too honest: 'the most innocent'.[6]

4 Jang and McClelland, *Stars between the Sun and Moon.*
5 Demick, *Nothing to Envy*, p. 142.
6 Ibid., pp. 140–141.

41. NORTH KOREA MAY BE UNDERGOING ANOTHER FAMINE

If you thought food shortages in North Korea couldn't get worse than the 1990s, think again. The country is no more arable than it used to be. People are still badly undernourished, particularly in areas far from Pyongyang where a current (2018) heat wave is withering staple crops, which could have 'potentially catastrophic effects', the International Federation of Red Cross and Red Crescent Societies told *Sky News*. Already, the society said, 25 per cent of children under the age of five are stunted by chronic malnutrition. It's sent emergency response teams to irrigate the hardest-hit fields and support 13,700 in two provinces deemed to be most at risk of running out of food.[1] An earlier drought lasted from March 2104 to July 2015, scorching the land and making it unable to absorb rain when typhoons hit during warm weather.

A 2017 report sponsored by the World Food Programme (WFP) reckons that approximately 18 million North Koreans, or 70 per cent, are 'in need', meaning all their food comes from government rations. In addition, 10.5 million are undernourished. One in five don't have access to clean water and sanitation.[2]

Here's an example of what happens to people who don't have access to clean water: in 2017, a North Korean soldier defected across the DMZ. His comrades shot him around five times, a violation of the official armistice. South Korean surgeons who operated on him discovered and removed several parasitic worms, one as long as 27 cm (10 inches).

---

1 'North Korean Heatwave Could Have "Catastrophic Effects", Charities Warn.' *Sky News*, 10 Aug. 2018, http://bit.ly/2wrGaEb.
2 Humanitarian Country Team in DPRK. *DPR Korea: Needs and Priorities*. March 2017.

'In my 20 years as a surgeon,' 'I have only seen something like this in a medical textbook.'[3]

Sanctions affect humanitarian aid as well as economic aid. Foreign aid workers agree that current sanctions have been hurting the most vulnerable in the population, not the elite in Pyongyang. Katharina Zellweger, who directs the Hong Kong-based KorAid, told the *South China Morning Post* that they are affecting 'the wrong people': children, pregnant women, the elderly, and people with disabilities. One of the worst results of the sanctions is losing access to a global fund that fights tuberculosis, which affects around 130,000 North Koreans.[4] Finally, the loss of Soviet agricultural assistance, particularly equipment, quality seeds, and fertiliser, has never been replaced since the fall of the USSR.

Financial and trade sanctions have worked to an extent in other countries. But North Korea has created a complex trade network that shields a lot of imports and exports, most of which are facilitated by China and Russia. Resources go to Pyongyang, which seems to be the only constituency that really matters in North Korea.

3 Westcott, Ben. 'What Parasitic Worms in Defector Reveal about North Korea.' CNN, 23 Nov. 2017.
4 Jeong-ho, Lee. 'Very Little Goes in': Aid for North Koreans Hampered by UN Sanctions. *South China Morning Post*, 27 June 2018, http://bit.ly/2wsjTWz.

42. STROKE AND CARDIOVASCULAR DISEASE KILL MORE THAN ONE-THIRD OF NORTH KOREANS

Heart disease is one thing North Koreans have in common with their Great and Dear Leaders. Kim Il-sung and Kim Jong-il both died from heart attacks, and cardiovascular disease and stroke are the top two causes of death in the country. Together, they amount to around 36 per cent of all deaths there. Data from the World Health Organisation shows the country ranks No. 4 in the world for stroke-related deaths.[1]

In addition, smoking rates are high in North Korea and are reflected in its worldwide ranking for lung disease (No. 3 in the world) and lung cancer (No. 2). They are the third and fifth most common causes for death in the country. Ri Yon-ok, a pharmacist who runs an anti-smoking campaign, told the Associated Press/CBC News that 54 per cent of adult Korean men smoke.[2] The World Health Organisation estimates a lower number – almost 44 per cent – but still pretty high. (To compare, the smoking rate in Great Britain and the US is less than 16 per cent.)

Few women smoke and it's illegal for anyone under seventeen to light up. But as we know, second-hand smoke can also cause lung disease and put non-smoking spouses and children at risk as well.

But why would heart disease be so prominent? Jeon Woo-taek and Kim So-yoon, two medical school professors from South Korea involved in 'reunification health', listed several problems in a 2017 interview with the *Korea Biomedical Review*. All the reasons can be traced to a

---

1 'Health Profile North Korea.' *World Life Expectancy*, 2017, http://bit.ly/2MPqxAE.
2 Talmadgee, Eric. 'North Korea Is Urging Its Men to Quit Smoking, and Women Are Leading the Charge.' *CBC News*, CBC/Radio Canada, 6 July 2016, http://bit.ly/2wsklUL.

lack of financial resources. Chronic food shortages, not enough vaccines and medicine, and poor water quality are the biggest threats to people's health, yet so necessary for heart patients to survive.[3] Add in unheated homes in winter, smokers everywhere, air pollution and a lot of infectious disease spread by unsanitary practices, even in hospitals, and the stage is set to weaken already strained and diseased hearts.

Infectious diseases are also common in North Korea. Hospitals routinely reuse syringes and needles, and sterilisation practices are poor. Hepatitis B is rampant in some areas; so are malaria and tuberculosis. Pneumonia rates are high, and pose a particular threat to people with advanced heart disease.

The famine – or rather, Arduous March – left many of its survivors with weakened organs, susceptible to any number of infectious diseases. Large swathes of the population outside Pyongyang remain undernourished (discussed in Fact 26) including many famine survivors. It's no wonder stroke rates are so high.

The South Korean doctors also say North Korea's health practices and standards are outdated. Ironically, North Korea sends many physicians to work in African nations to gain experience and send back money (the state keeps 80 per cent of their earnings).

---

3 Williams, Constance. 'North Korea's Healthcare System Desperately Needs South's Help.' *Korea Biomedical Review*, 27 July 2017, http://bit.ly/2NlHi3l.

43. Famine Changed North Korean Society and Made Women the Chief Breadwinners

Many of the survivors of the 1990s famine were women, and they shaped an underground economy that became part of North Korean life.

As Barbara Demick says, North Korean women truly were the 'Mothers of Invention'. Thousands of women became self-employed to sustain themselves and their families. There were no jobs to go to, as factories shut down and even worksites that were still open were unable to pay salaries or distribute food ration coupons. So women created their own businesses and sold what they could make or bake. They helped create open-air markets in empty spaces, with tacit approval from local governments.

More women than men survived the famine because they needed fewer calories to get by. One of Demick's subjects was married to a large chap (by North Korean standards) who weakened and died as his body was unable to convert energy from the little food his wife could get. Their son, an elite athlete who had attended a boxing school, lost so much muscle he literally wasted away.

People who managed to survive made shoes and essential household items from scraps of whatever materials they could find. Others read up on traditional medicine and established herbal treatment practices. Many people bartered for products and services. Physicians, unpaid like everyone else, accepted rice or coal in exchange for providing medical documentation to stay away from 'work' (some jobsites remained open to keep up appearances) or to perform minor surgeries outside the hospital.

Demick's widowed subject and her daughter took to baking cookies, a useful and lightweight sale item. They hoarded milk and sugar and baked their cookies in different shapes to stand out from the competition. Plus, they were natural salespeople who attracted customers.

Later, as foreign food aid came in and was resold at these open-air black markets, people became a little bolder. Farmers came to sell vegetables grown in hidden gardens or out-of-the-way mountainsides. There was also a healthy demand for smuggled Chinese goods, the result of Premier Deng Xiaoping's economic reforms. Demick's subject saw oranges and pineapples for the first time, as well as colourful, affordable clothing.

As the markets grew, other businesses opened. Men put together wagons to deliver large items to local homes; the wagons also provided a handy place to sleep. Barbers and beauticians set up shop, gaining more customers as more people could afford to treat themselves.

This was quite a transformation: not only were North Koreans providing for themselves – anathema in a strictly Communist country – but women were largely leading it, albeit quietly. Joo Sung-ha, a North Korean who defected and is now a writer in the South, told Demick that he believes Kim Jong-il decided not to contest the markets. 'If [married women] hadn't been allowed to work, there would have been a revolution.'[1] Assuming, of course, that anyone had the energy to get up and revolt.

1 Demick, Barbara, *Nothing to Envy*, p. 167.

44. The Famine Created a New Class of Orphans

Normally, North Koreans are restricted to their hometowns or provinces and must obtain travel permits to go outside the area. This system broke down during the famine, resulting in widespread abandonment of homes and children.

As famine spread to affect even some of the elite classes, more children were left at state-run orphanages by their desperate parents; others wandered around until they were picked up by the authorities and placed in the orphanages, creating a whole new class of orphans: 'wandering swallows', or kochebi.

Many kochebi left the orphanages when the food ran out. They joined adults also on the move in search of work and food. In fact, during the famine much of North Korea was constantly moving; to stay still was to allow yourself to starve.

Kochebi often hung around train stations where they sometimes got new clothes handed out by government workers who weren't actively stealing foreign aid. Their primary activity, though, was begging. As fewer people had anything to share, they resorted to scouring the grounds for leftover food or spillage. They took to smoking discarded cigarette butts to get some relief from hunger pangs.

Older children who had a bit more energy and the ability to fight for food learned how to distract food vendors. Some would rush a stand and knock it over while their pals scooped up food for the gang. Others watched incoming trains that might be hauling food, or jumped on slow-moving ones where they would hunt for food and other goods, slitting open sacks and hauling off what they could in bags. The authorities responded by stationing soldiers with orders to shoot and kill anyone seen stealing food from trains.

Most of the younger kochebi probably died from starvation or disease. One of Demick's sources recalled seeing little children around the train stations each morning and walking by their dead bodies later in the day. Many weren't strong enough to fight for food, while others fell prey to violent predators. Some defectors reported that kochebi were killed and cannibalised.

Demick's sources told her it wasn't at all unusual for people to die on trains en route to a new destination. Railway station workers removed bodies found on trains, and in and around railroad stations, each day and buried them in mass graves. In a Confucian society, this is particularly damning because it is believed that a loved one's burial place can determine his or her survivors' fortunes.

Sadly, there are still reports of homeless children in North Korea. In her memoir about her year teaching at the Christian-run Pyongyang University of Science and Technology, journalist Suki Kim writes about a school administrator who purchased and surreptitiously distributed small rice cakes to 'homeless kids who roamed the market and picked pockets'.[1]

---

1 Kim, *Without You, There Is No Us,* pp. 219–220.

45. Before the Famine, North Korea Took Pretty Good Care of Its Citizens

Part of the reason the famine was so devastating is that up until the 1980s, the North Korean government took pretty good care of its citizens.

In the 1960s and '70s, North Korean defector Yeonmi Park writes, 'the state took care of everyone's basic needs: clothes, medical care, food.' But after the Communist bloc crumpled, she says, 'North Koreans were suddenly on their own ... our state-controlled economy collapsed.'[1] Later, after she escaped to South Korea, Park was amazed to learn that before the famine, most people received 700 g of grain every day. During the famine, an entire family would be lucky to get that much for a week.

Soviet support had already been dwindling since Stalin's death in 1953. His successor, Nikita Khrushchev, advocated 'de-Stalinisation' and ending leadership cults. This strained Sino-Soviet relations to the point that a 'Sino-Soviet' split was evident by 1960. Kim Il-sung tried to balance relations with both nations. At the time, North Korea was doing pretty well; a 1994 study by the US Army concluded that the focus on heavy industry brought record growth to the nation's coffers during the 1950s and 1960s.

But this strategy floundered in the 1970s as the country's infrastructure and industrial equipment began to age and break down. To raise funds, North Korea sold bonds worth $2–$3 billion on the international market to continue funding its needs – a very capitalistic solution![2]

While few people lived well, no one was starving. Park remembers her family used to buy noodles to share with

---

1 Park and Vollers, *In Order to Live*, p.15.
2 Department of the Army, *North Korea: a Country Study*. Federal Research Division, Library of Congress, 1994, pp. 40-41, http://bit.ly/2P6un60.

friends, and families grew vegetables in their own gardens. In some parts of the country, people could even purchase local food. But the government controlled distribution of grains such as rice and maize, which provided most of the calories in the North Korean diet. The government allocated grains through coupons or vouchers usually given at worksites or inminban, local 'People's Groups' that assigned communal work and monitored local events and behaviours (discussed in Fact 23).

Children received biscuits on their birthdays 'from Kim Il-sung', who would also provide useful, if random, items such as toys, books and clothing from time to time through coupons distributed by local authorities. In other words, the government did just enough to keep people reasonably content. As they were entirely cut off from the outside world, they didn't sneer at the occasional gift of a bra or set of drinking cups.

The higher a family's songbun status, the better stuff they received. Kim bestowed record players, radios, and TV sets. Soldiers enjoyed oranges, a rare treat for most people. The idea was to create a cashless society, putatively independent as Juche demanded, but dependent on their father-God leader for just about everything.

46. Just 3 Million People Are Permitted to Live in Pyongyang

Pyongyang is a city for North Korea's elite and those who serve them.

Suki Kim writes that there are two distinct sets of people in Pyongyang: those who are 'well fed and had healthy complexions and were of regular height' and 'all other people' she glimpsed from occasional bus trips from her job as an English instructor at Pyongyang University of Science and Technology (PUST). These people were 'often bony, their faces dark green from overexposure to the sun or malnutrition or something worse. They were generally shorter and markedly smaller in every way.'[1]

It's rare for someone from a lower songbun to be permitted to travel or study in Pyongyang, but not altogether impossible. One of the defectors Barbara Demick interviewed grew up in the northern industrial city of Chongjin and was accepted into Pyongyang's Kim Chaek University of Technology. Not only was this young man from the 'wrong' region, his parents were Japanese-born Koreans, or kitachosenjin. While such Koreans were officially welcomed, they are viewed with some degree of suspicion and some were purged in the 1970s.

Students at Pyongyang's elite universities (Kim Il-sung University, Kim Chaek, and PUST) have access to resources rarely seen outside the capital city. Demick's Kim Chaek alumnus read translated Western literature including *Gone With the Wind* (his favourite), *One Hundred Years of Solitude*, and even the 1930s self-help classic *How to Win Friends and Influence People*. His classmates, most from privileged families, loaned him books and magazines they or their families brought back from foreign travels.

1 Kim, *Without You, There Is No Us*, p. 101.

Students at these elite universities were also prioritised to receive adequate food during the famine.

In terms of appearance, South Korean historian Yuhwan Koh divides Pyongyang architecture into three phases that roughly reflect the influence of each Kim.

Massive housing complexes and government buildings mark the Kim Il-sung era. These construction projects, largely funded by the Soviet Union, helped North Korea remain economically superior to the South until the 1980s, when Kim Jong-il began taking over more projects.

Kim Jong-il's era featured grandiose projects like the Ryugyong Hotel, a 105-storey pyramid high-rise that was never finished or opened for business. (Regardless, it was the world's tallest hotel until 2009 and is the tallest unoccupied building in the world.) This was also when boulevards decked with monuments were constructed, and new or renovated public places rose, such as the Juche Tower, Kim Il-sung Stadium, and Rungrado 1st of May Stadium.

The present Kim's era has so far been more colourful and user-friendly. Statues have been lacquered and varnished to look more like Madame Tussaud exhibits, observes architectural writer Owen Hatherley, and there are more places to buy groceries, eat, and just get coffee.[2]

2 Hatherley, Owen. 'What is it like to live in Pyongyang? Two recent events explored "ordinary life" in the city.' *Prospect*, 16 November 2017, http://bit.ly/2PAZHdY.

47. PYONGYANG IS FOR FASHIONISTAS!

Budding fashionistas will be reasonably comfortable in Pyongyang, as long as they can live without jeans and are fine with Duchess Kate tastes favoured by the city's alpha 'nista, Ri Sol-ju, the wife of Kim Jong-un.

Even if 'Squeak' were to appear in jeans, Ri wouldn't wear them in public because her husband is keeping up the ban on Western things like jeans, T-shirts, blue or pink hair dye, and piercings following a reported crackdown in the border areas in 2017, where people were spotted wearing branded clothing. Since most North Koreans are barely getting by, fashion isn't something they think about for their day-to-day survival. But in Pyongyang, things are getting a little South Ken, even if clothes are still made from vynalon, a stiff and dye-resistant synthetic fibre that's been produced there since the 1950s, an important part of Juche self-reliance.

We can thank Ri for that. She started stepping out in 2012 to alert the world of the presence of a Mrs Kim. Since then she's updated her wardrobe and often accompanies her husband to 'soft' venues that don't have missiles, like cosmetic and clothing factories and a K-pop concert. She didn't even wear a Kim pin at the opening of the Rungna People's Pleasure Ground amusement park; instead, she wore a brooch.

Like Kate, she wears a lot of contrasting monochrome outfits, polka-dot dresses, and subtly coloured two-piece suits. The *South China Morning Post* notes that she's as label-driven as any high-ranking North Korean, with preferences 'documented on camera' for Dior, Movado, and Tiffany, and these ain't knock-offs.[1]

---

1 'North Korean First Lady's Fashion Choices Open Elite's Eyes to Glamour.' *South China Morning Post*, 1 Dec. 2017, http://bit. ly/2MRafaj.

Carol Giacomo, a former Reuter's diplomatic correspondent who now sits on *The New York Times'* editorial board, visited Pyongyang in 2017 to attend its thirteenth International Trade Fair. She was surprised by the amount of colour she saw, and not just on traditional Korean dress. Chanel-style suits in pinks, purples, and white were seen almost as often as black and white, and 'skirts often ride slightly above the knee.'[2] Open-toed heels were not only tolerated, but women walked in them, for *miles*, something Bridget Jones and even Carrie Bradshaw couldn't manage.

Kim, we've seen, dresses in Armani and is bold enough to wear fedoras in cold weather and Panama-style hats with casual outfits when it's warmer. Other men dressed less colourfully, although Giacomo noticed a foreign ministry official who added a blue tie with white polka dots to his black suit and white dress shirt. Children also add a touch of personalisation in their school uniforms with colourful backpacks, socks, and for girls, platform shoes and ruffled shirts. And as Wendy Simmons noticed during her photo tour of North Korea, toddlers wore the most colourful clothing, 'a riot of pattern and hue'.

2 Giacomo, Carol. 'Decoding Dress in North Korea.' *The New York Times*, 16 Oct. 2017, https://nyti.ms/2NlzRsO.

48. Hair Styles Are Strictly Limited in North Korea and No One Can Have Kim Jong-un's Style

Men and women in North Korea are limited to fifteen approved hairstyles for each gender. No one, however, can sport the same cut as Kim Jong-un.

The options for men offer a lot less variety than women, who at least have a couple of styles that allow hair to grow just past the shoulders. Men are expected to keep their hair well above the collar, but they can shave the sides à la Kim. Hair cannot be dyed with a contrasting colour, such as blue or pink.

Not surprisingly, North Koreans are prohibited from getting body piercings and wearing Western clothing. *The Guardian* reports that parts of the country are subject to teen-run inspection units[1] reminiscent of other youth-led enforcement units like Mao's Red Guard and Iran's Revolutionary Guard.

Dennis Rodman, a former basketball player in the US, who is pals with Kim Jong-un, is apparently exempt from all these rules. Rodman has sported wild hair colours, piercings, ripped clothing – trappings of a wealthy ex-athlete – when visiting Pyongyang.

Tattoos are permitted if they praise the Kim family or have some other approved message. One defector told *The Guardian* that his father's generation often had slogans tattooed on their arms. Bears, dragons, eagles, and doves are also popular.[2]

---

1 Rothwell, James. 'North Korea Bans Piercings and Western-Style Clothing.' *The Telegraph*, 17 Apr. 2016, http://bit.ly/2BO1lpI.
2 Bell, Markus. 'Fatherland! Victory! Battle!' – Tattoos in North Korea.' *The Guardian*, 29 Jan. 2015, http://bit.ly/2oeErhM.

49. KIM IL-SUNG'S FIRST MARRIAGE WAS PROBABLY FOR LOVE

North Korea's first leader, Kim Il-sung, was married twice: first to a woman who joined his guerrilla band in her teens, and later to a former secretary who quickly rose in Party ranks.

Kim's first wife was Kim Jong-suk. Born Christmas Day 1917 to poor farmers in present-day North Korea, she moved from Korea to Manchuria as a child. She was soon orphaned and later joined Kim Il-sung's guerillas as a kitchen helper when she was around sixteen. In 1937, the Japanese arrested her for stealing food for her hungry comrades.

After her release, she rejoined the group, now in the Soviet Union. Kim probably knew her from the guerrilla days (after all, his band was hardly a large one) and was no doubt impressed by her determination to return to them after her release from prison.

The two married in 1941. She gave birth to their son Kim Jong-il later that year, or possibly in 1942. In 1944, another son was born, Kim Man-il. Both boys were given Russian names: Yuri Irsenovich Kim, or Yura for Jong-il, and Alexander, or Shura, for the younger boy. And in 1946, a daughter, Kim Kyong-hui, was born; she apparently didn't rate a Russian name. Kim Kyong-hui, who holds the title 'General', was married to General Jang Sung-taek, who was executed in 2013 by their nephew Kim Jong-un.

Kim Man-il drowned in 1947 or 1948, shortly before the family joined Kim in Korea. At least one source, former CIA political psychologist Jerrold Post, believes Man-il was forcibly drowned by Jong-il during rough play.[1] (Disclaimer: Dr Post was one of my professors at The George Washington University.)

1 Post, Jerrold M. "Kim Jong-il of North Korea: in the Shadow of His Father." Wiley/Blackwell (10.1111), 20 Aug. 2008, http://bit.ly/2PD0MBY.

Photos of Kim Jong-suk show a tiny woman. Her husband, who was 5 feet 9 inches, towered over her; later, official portraits show her to be much closer to his height. Her official biography lauds her marksmanship skills and says she used them to save Kim Il-sung's life, an unlikely scenario given the fact that she worked as a camp follower (albeit an unusually devoted one) and women were stuck in very traditional roles. You can watch a 2007 documentary about her called *Your Mother's Gun Will Last Forever* at http://bit.ly/2LonsCR, where there are indeed a lot of images of Kim with her gun. There are, alas, no subtitles.

The official biography says her greatest achievement was bringing up Kim Jong-il. She was also known for cooking enormous meals to feed visiting Soviet generals and other VIPs her husband wanted to impress.

North Korea observed the 100th anniversary of her birth in 2017 with cultural performances and released new stamps and coins with her image. She died in Pyongyang in 1949, probably from complications resulting from stillbirth. The cause of death is not given in her official biography, although at the time it was said that she died from the lasting effects of a hard guerrilla life. It's possible that she also had tuberculosis.

50. Kim Il-sung's Second Wife Was the First North Korean Woman to Hold Real Power

Kim Il-sung remarried twenty-eight-year-old Pyongyang native Kim Song-ae in 1952. At the time of the marriage, she had been working as a secretary. Because the Korean War was still going on at the time of the marriage, there was no formal ceremony or celebration.

The couple had three children:

Daughter Kim Kyong-jin, born in 1952 or 1953. She is married to North Korea's long-time Ambassador to Austria.

Son Kim Pyong-il, born 1954 and named for Kim Il-sung's son who died young in the Soviet Union. He has been serving as North Korea's Ambassador to the Czech Republic since 2015.

Son Kim Yong-il, born 1955 or 1957. He is believed to have died in Germany around 2000.

Like many women, Kim Song-ae went back to work when her children were young. In her case, she mirrored the power given to Jiang Qing – also known as Madame Mao – by her husband, the Chinese leader Mao Zedung. This made her the first woman to wield real power in North Korea.

First, she was named vice-chairwoman of the Korean Democratic Women's League (KWDL) in 1965. In 1971, she became the chairwoman. The following year she became a representative in the People's Supreme Assembly, the nation's legislature.

It didn't take long for 'Mrs Kim' to annoy her fellow legislators, particularly her campaign to have her son Kim Pyong-il succeed her husband. Her brother-in-law Kim Yong-ju and her own brother Kim Kwang-hop supported her. This created an obvious conflict with her stepson Kim Jong-il, who had little love for his stepmother to begin with.

He and his supporters began to put the brakes on her power grab, starting with taking away the KWDL chairmanship in 1974. His own succession firmly in place, Kim Jong-il put her and her brother under house arrest in 1981.

She joined her husband to meet with former US President Jimmy Carter when he visited North Korea in 1994, which was her last public appearance. She is said to have supported Carter's request for the remains of US soldiers to be repatriated. But as her stepson's influence grew, her roles shrank. By the time her husband died in 1994, she was listed No. 103 on his funeral committee, a very public and serious snub.

Kim Jong-il, who produced dozens of North Korean films, memorialised his stepmother in one called *Our Family's Problem* about a good man with an evil wife. The actress who played the wife was said to have had a strong resemblance to Kim Song-ae.

Kim Song-ae pretty much disappeared from public mention after 1998, which of course led to lots of rumours about her. One had her killed in a car accident in Beijing in 2001. A defector later claimed she had been declared insane before Kim Il-sung died. To this day, it is not certain if she is still alive; if she were, she would be in her mid-nineties.

51. KIM IL-SUNG MET WITH THE LEADER OF A CULT CHURCH YEARS BEFORE THE SUNSHINE POLICY

Years before South Korean President Kim Dae-jung launched his 'sunshine policy' with North Korea in 1998, Sun Myung-moon, a charismatic religious leader and head of an arguably cultish church met with Kim Il-sung in 1991. Kim's vice premier and chairman of the country's external economic commission invited him in a fairly obvious appeal for investment.

Moon and Kim could not have been more different in outlook, but they had some interesting similarities:

Both were born in present-day North Korea during the Japanese occupation.

Both were from families that practised Christianity.

Both saw themselves as saviours: Kim for Korea, Moon for the world.

Both were political prisoners at one time.

Sun Myung-moon (1920–2012) founded the Holy Spirit for the Unification of World Christianity in 1954 in Seoul, also called the Unification Church. It is probably best known for conducting mass weddings that unite thousands of couples in one ceremony. Moon proclaimed himself the Messiah, and his church grew during a wave of alternative religions that flourished during the 1960s and '70s, particularly in the West.

Moon, who began preaching in his late teens after receiving a vision, became an ardent anti-Communist in the years after the war – not a good thing in North Korea. He was imprisoned in a labour camp and may have been tortured. After his release in 1950, he fled to South Korea.

In 1972, he moved the church's operations from Seoul to the US. Many observers here regard the Unification Church as a cult, but Moon's conservative outlook attracted support from conservative politicians in the US, including President Richard Nixon.

During the 1980s, Moon served eighteen months in a US prison for tax evasion and briefly turned on the country, saying it had persecuted him. (He also complained about American women and gay people.) And yet he had regained a lot of his stature by 1991. His media company had launched the extremely conservative newspaper *The Washington Times* in Washington DC in 1982 and bought United Press International (UPI), a major news service in 2000 that's now quite small compared to its heyday.

Kim no doubt saw meeting with Moon as a potential to get hard currency, and he was right. During the 1990s, Moon bankrolled North Korean industry, particularly Pyeonghwa Motors, a joint company co-owned by the church and North Korea that operates to this day. It's the only company in North Korea permitted to advertise, and it (probably) only has one competitor: Pyongchang Auto Works. Like many Koreans, Moon wanted to see a unified Korea, although the rhetoric from his media rarely followed suit.

The South Korean government was not pleased with Moon's foray into foreign relations and saw it as destabilising. They must have seethed when the media, relying on church sources, reported that Kim asked Moon to arrange a visit to the US to meet with President George H. W. Bush, a request that was never fulfilled.

52. The Founder of Hyundai Delivered 'Unification Cows' to North Korea

In 1998, Chung Ju-young, the elderly founder of Hyundai Group, headed a cattle drive of some 500 'unification cows' (actually, male and female cattle) from South Korea into the North. The gesture came about after an appeal from South Korea's President Kim Dae-jung.

The newly elected Kim wanted to try a more pragmatic, 'sunshine policy' approach to North Korean relations, starting with gift-giving, a traditional Korean way to soften relations with enemies. (Kim, who consulted with the British writer and artist Elizabeth Young, Lady Kennet, on this tactic, went on to be awarded the Nobel Peace Prize for his efforts.) He asked the country's leading businesspeople to act as ambassadors to the North. The Northern-born Chung took that directive to heart, according to *The New York Times*.[1]

Seventy-five years earlier, Chung had left his family's farm in the village of Tongchong in what is present-day North Korea for Seoul. To help him along the way, he took a couple of cows to sell. Those cows funded a pretty good investment. Hyundai Motors is South Korea's second-largest business behind Samsung, and is ranked at 78 on the Fortune Global 500. In addition to being the world's third-largest car manufacturer, Hyundai is involved in construction, IT, energy, finance, and heavy industry. It manufactures vehicles for the railway and defence industries and has a huge presence in auto parts manufacturing. For a while it tried to compete with Samsung in the electronics market; my very first desktop was a hard-working Hyundai.

---

1 Strom, Stephanie. 'In Drive for Unity, Hyundai Founder Takes Cattle to North Korea.' *The New York Times*, 17 June 1998, https://nyti.ms/2OMo4Ee.

Being a successful businessman means you'd be a great president, right? Chung ran for the South Korean presidency in 1992, delivering a platform attacking the economic policies of the incumbent president Roh Tae-woo, who had reached term limits. He got 16 per cent of the vote and Kim Young-sam was elected. And for all his efforts, Chung was charged with embezzlement and received a suspended sentence. This hurt Hyundai's ability to get financing for several years.

The cattle drive was a symbolic way for Chung to ask all of North Korea to forgive his theft and perhaps his later judgment lapses. As *The Washington Post* described it, Chung led a fifty-truck convey from a black limousine. As he entered Imjingak, the last village before the DMZ, he was greeted by 'thousands of well-wishers including Buddhist monks and women in traditional pink dress'. Then, at the DMZ:

> the extremely frail Chung, aided by a cane and a helper holding each arm, stepped out of his car ... and shuffled 30 yards across the frontier – the first civilian since World War II to make that crossing without a government escort.[2]

As far as I can tell, no one else has since crossed the border without an escort.

2 Sullivan, Kevin. 'S. Korean Auto Tycoon Drives Cattle To North.' *The Washington Post*, 17 June 1998, https://wapo.st/2nQ4v2k.

53. KIM JONG-IL MAY HAVE STRESSED HIS FATHER INTO A HEART ATTACK

Imagine you've set up a hereditary dictatorship and your heir is running the economy so you can get your hands on plutonium, while angling for a summit with your neighbour and arch-enemy. You read the economic reports, make a few comments, and go back to angering a world power. It can be stressful, particularly when you learn the kid has tanked the economy.

This is pretty much how Kim Il-sung spent his last months before he died in 1994. In late June, the Kims retreated to a remote villa. They argued about an upcoming summit with South Korea and whether the father should greet President Kim Young-sam at the airport.

In addition, the Great Leader was pretty angry that he hadn't been given an accurate picture of the economy and food shortages in the provinces, where they had become severe.

Kim & Son argued, a lot, and apparently the father suffered a heart attack and was found dead and alone. As Victor Cha notes, this was unusual for someone who travelled with a medical squad and was rarely by himself for more than a few minutes.[1]

It's also odd that Kim's regular physician was absent and replaced by an inexperienced doctor. Even more suspicious is that everyone who was at the compound that day died mysteriously or disappeared except, of course, Kim Jong-il.

Did Kim II plan to isolate Kim I and literally stress him into a heart attack?

---

1 Cha, *The Impossible State*, pp. 90-91.

54. The Kims Purge Advisors, Appointees, and Family

All three Great Leaders have purged or executed high-ranking individuals to reinforce their power.

Kim Il-sung learned from the best: Josef Stalin. The songbun caste system Kim created, discussed in Fact 24, produced an environment where fear became a normal part of life. At the same time, the populace was essentially brainwashed to believe that their well-being depended entirely on him.

During the years leading up to the Korean War, Kim Il-sung killed leading socialists, Communists, and well-placed bureaucrats he viewed as potential challengers. After the war, he focused on three factions who either publicly challenged him or he suspected of plotting against him:

The Domestic Faction, Koreans who were active in the underground Communist movement during Japanese rule.

The Yan'an Faction who left Korea in the 1920s and 1930s and followed Chinese Communist leaders to their headquarters in Yan'an (also called Shaanxi) Province.

The Soviet Korean Faction, ethnic Koreans born in the Soviet Union.[1]

Kim moved against the Yan'an and Soviet factions in the mid-1950s after a Yan'an leader explicitly criticised his 'police state' while he was, ironically, in the Soviet Union where Stalin's successor, Nikita Khrushchev, ordered him to end the personality cult.

Upon returning to Pyongyang, Kim promised reforms and a moderate approach in exchange for re-election as Party chairman. Then he expelled leading Yan'an politicians

1 'Northern Korean Purges – Kim Il-sung.' http://bit.ly/2BRAJ7q.

and purged others. Many simply disappeared, including President Kim Tu-bong a member of the Yan'an faction. Other politicians fled the country to avoid arrest. Kim briefly stopped his purges after the Soviets and Chinese had a kind of intervention and even pardoned some enemies he had arrested and imprisoned. But by 1961, the only real faction left in North Korea was his own.

Kim Jong-il also purged Party members early in his rule, starting with the Sixth Army Corps in 1995, less than a year after his father died. He may have executed more than 100 soldiers and officers accused of embezzlement. In 1997, he executed the Party secretary in charge of agriculture, assigning him blame for the famine and spying for the US Around the same time, he executed around 2,000 more people he said had been spies during the war that had ended thirty-five years earlier. Their families were also purged – executed or imprisoned.

Not long before his death, Kim sent around 100 senior Party officials to firing squads, ostensibly for failing to implement currency reform. Another sixty aides were publicly executed, a warning not to challenge his son Kim Jong-un.

Kim Jong-un's targets included older, high-ranking officials including his own uncle. He had him arrested and executed in 2013. In 2015, he executed his former defence chief. And in February 2017, two women were hired for what they thought was a prank on his older half-brother, Kim Jong-nam, at the Kuala Lumpur International Airport. The prank resulted in his death from a nerve agent. Read more about this event in Fact 63.

55. There Have Been Assassination Attempts on the Kims

Kim Jong-un was said to have been worried about potential assassination attempts before meeting with Donald Trump in 2018. He certainly had good reason: throughout North Korea's history, there have been assassination attempts against the Kims.

In 2013, a Pyongyang 'Traffic Lady' was given one of the nation's highest honours for actions that foiled an assassination attempt against Kim Jong-un. It appears she had stopped and searched a vehicle that was supposed to launch a series of actions beginning with a staged traffic accident while Kim was travelling in the area. (Fact 85 discusses the iconic 'Traffic Ladies'.)

Kim Il-sung was nearly assassinated in 1946 when a South Korean agent tossed a grenade at him; a Soviet Army lieutenant picked it up in time to throw it away, according to an account from the NATO Association of Canada.[1] There were also assassination attempts on Syngman Rhee, South Korea's first president, and both nations have been complicit in attempts to kill each other's leaders.

In 2004, two trains loaded with fuel and possibly ammonium nitrate exploded at a train station close to the border with China, killing fifty-four people and injuring more than 1,200. The Red Cross was permitted into the area and reported that the explosion was so powerful some debris blasted over into China. Kim Jong-il had passed through the station hours earlier as he returned home from meetings in China, leading to speculation that the explosion may have been targeted at him. It was later found that a live power cable had contact with a fuel leak and triggered

1 Jung, Daniel. 'South Korean Special Forces Attempted to Assassinate Kim Il-sung.' NAOC, 30 Sept. 2017, http://bit.ly/2oeIfzv.

the explosion. It's also possible that Kim's travel mixed up some railroad communications; certainly Kim believed it. According to Thae Yong-ho, a diplomat who defected to London in 2016, Kim ordered the execution of the country's railroads chief and other transportation officials.

In 2017, North Korea unleashed an unusually detailed account of an attempt on Kim Jong-un's life by the US and South Korea, which it alleged had bribed and recruited a North Korean working in Russia. The worker, who North Korean media reported received $20,000 and training from South Korea's National Intelligence Service, was supposed to attack Kim with a delayed-action biochemical weapon during a military parade.

That year, as Kim strutted around the launch pad at the Punggye-ri nuclear test site on 4 July (which happens to be Independence Day in the US), satellites put him in clear sight of US military and intelligence personnel for more than an hour. According to *The Independent*, they watched him smoke[2] – probably not such a great idea around so much rocket fuel – and walk just a few feet away from the missile.

2 Lockie, Alex. 'The US Had a Clear Shot at Killing Kim Jong-un on 4 July – Here's Why It Didn't Strike.' *The Independent*, 12 July 2017, https://ind.pn/2KZQp7P.

56. Kim Jong-il Took Hedonism to New Levels

Kim Jong-il lived a lifestyle that reminds me of the way Caligula's was portrayed in *I Claudius*. While Kim Il-sung established 'Joy Divisions' of young women trained to entertain him and high officials, his son took hedonism to new levels.

Kim Jong-il may have had as many as thirteen children. And as thousands of Koreans died from starvation and disease, he lived ostentatiously, to put it mildly. He had ten palaces with golf courses, indoor pools, horse stables, basketball courts, and wine cellars stocked with rare wines. His sushi chef, Kenji Fujimoto, wrote of four-day banquets and Joy Division women who bathed him; he once ordered them to dance naked with his guests.[1]

At the height of the famine, as his countrymen ate grass, Kim imported $2.6 millions' worth of Swiss watches and he once paid $20 million for 200 Mercedes S-class limousines.[2]

His son and one-time heir Kim Jong-nam didn't fall too far from the tree. He preferred the globetrotting life to establishing domestic pleasure palaces and owned villas in China and Macau. Like his father, he enjoyed fast cars, gambling, and alcohol. Unlike his father, he loved jewellery and designer jeans. It's thought that he had two wives, at least one mistress, and four to six children. He seemed pleased with the international playboy label.[3]

1   Watts, Jonathan. 'Chef Serves up Kim's Life of Sushi and Orgy.' *The Guardian*, 19 July 2003, http://bit.ly/2P7dF6n.
2   Cha, *The Impossible State*, p. 81.
3   Ibid, p. 97.

57. Kim Jong-il's Progeny Are Numerous

Kim Jong-il certainly had a complicated life. As Victor Cha put it in his book *The Impossible State*, it 'reads like a script from The Sopranos'.[1]

Kim Il-sung arranged his son's marriage, as traditional Korean parents will do. The first (and official) wife was Kim Young-sook, the daughter of a Workers' Party official. Their only child, Kim Sol-song (born 1974), worked in the country's propaganda department and directed literary affairs. She was reported to be Kim's favourite child.

It's possible that Kim Young-sook was actually Kim's second wife. Some claim his first was the daughter of a soldier who died in the Korean War. They divorced after two years and may have had a daughter.

Kim took up with North Korean film star Song Hye-rim. She was married, so he had her husband sent to France, according to Cha. Their son, Kim Jong-nam (born 1971), died in a nerve gas attack at a Malaysian airport reportedly arranged by his younger half-brother, the current Supreme Leader.

After Song, Kim's eye next fell upon a Japanese-born Korean dancer, Ko Yong-hui, who held the title First Lady until her death from cancer in 2004. They had two sons, Kim Jong-chul (born 1981) and Kim Jong-un (born 1983). A daughter, Kim Yo-jong, was born in the late 1980s; she is close to Kim Jong-un and represented him at the 2018 South Korean Olympics.

Cha writes that Kim had other mistresses and nine other children.

---

1 Cha, *The Impossible State*, p. 83.

58. Kim Jong-il Saw Himself as a Master Filmmaker

Kim Jong-il was fascinated by film and television and owned more than 30,000 films. He produced or was a consultant for nearly 12,000 films, most of which have never been shown outside North Korea. He loved Western film: the *Bond* series (at least until *Die Another Day*) and *Rambo*, *Friday the 13th*, and the *Godzilla* films. He also owned every Oscar-winning film and, it's said, a lot of pornography.

Of course, very few North Koreans can see films made outside North Korea. At best, they can watch smuggled copies – at great risk to themselves and their families.

Kim seems to have stumbled on film on his own. His secondary schooling blended subjects such as Marxist political theory with practical applications like mechanics (including automotive repair). Later, at Kim Il-sung University, he majored in Marxist political economy but also took classes in television broadcasting.

After graduating in 1964, Kim was put in charge of the country's Publicity and Information (i.e., propaganda) Department. This was a particularly important role since the other major Communist powers – the Soviet Union and China – were clashing over ideological differences. Kim Il-sung wanted to keep North Korea out of the debate and focus on ensuring 'burning loyalty' to himself and through him, his son. Propaganda was essential to keep foreign ideas out of the Juche Nation.

Kim Jong-il used film to spread burning loyalty, adherence to Juche principles, and emphasise official North Korean history (alternative facts, if you will). There were even movies for the kids to enjoy, according to the BBC, which reported back in 2011 that a sign outside the Ministry of Culture declared 'Make More Cartoons.'[1]

Kim ordered writers, artists and media officials to include official ideology in their work. But he wanted film to lead other arts. He wrote several books and essays on filmmaking and in 1973, he published a propaganda manifesto, *On the Art of the Cinema*, to explain why focusing on cinema should be part of any revolutionary's toolkit. It quickly became required reading for all film students in North Korea.

You can purchase this on Amazon, where 69 per cent of reviewers gave it five stars and reviews that I have to assume are ironic. If you want to read more without buying the book, see Luke Bather's article for *Mental Floss*, '10 Filmmaking Lessons from Kim Jong-il' at http://bit.ly/2MxmNo2.

In 1987, Kim published an essay on directing just a year after the South Korean director Shin Sang-ok and his wife, actress Choi Eun-hui, escaped after being held in North Korea for eight years, which is discussed in Fact 59.

Interestingly, while Kim micromanaged North Korea's film industry, he did not require that each film extol North Korea and its leaders. But, according to one actress who managed to escape North Korea, they were instructed as to what they could and couldn't wear, and were even told what make-up to use.[1]

---

1 Savage, Mark. 'Kim Jong-il: The Cinephile Despot.' *BBC News*, 19 Dec. 2011, https://bbc.in/2Mx22Zw.

59. Kim Jong-il Kidnapped a South Korean Director and Actress Who Later Defected to the United States

The 1978 kidnapping of two popular South Korean cinema stars at Kim Jong-il's behest may be one of the best-known facts to leak out of North Korea.

Choi Eun-hui was one of the most popular stars of South Korean cinema in the 1960s and 1970s. She married Shin Sang-ok, a respected film director, in 1954. The two had been divorced at the time of their separate kidnappings, remarried at Kim's urging, and after convincing their handlers that they had 'burning loyalty' to the regime, defected to the US embassy in Vienna in 1984 while on an official state visit.

Choi divorced Shin in 1976 after she discovered he had two other children with a younger actress. The divorce, and perhaps her age (she was forty at the time) hurt her career. So when a businessman asked her to meet him in Hong Kong in January 1978 to discuss starting a new film company, she jumped at the opportunity. But it was a kidnapping set-up arranged by Kim Jong-il, who was North Korea's Minister of Culture at the time.

Later that year, her ex-husband travelled to Hong Kong to investigate her abduction and to clear his name in tabloid papers. He, too, was kidnapped.

Choi lived in a luxurious Pyongyang villa and was assigned a tutor to re-educate her. Kim Jong-il took her to parties, opera, theatre, and other cultural events.

Shin initially was given equally nice accommodations upon his arrival in Pyongyang. However, he tried to escape several times and was sent to Prison Number 6. There, he later said, he subsisted on ideology classes, grass, rice, and salt for four years until he was deemed suitably re-educated and released.[1]

In 1983, Kim reunited Shin with Choi at a dinner party. Each had been unaware that the other was in North Korea. They were equally surprised, Shin wrote in his autobiography, that Kim kidnapped them to reinvent North Korean cinema. 'The North's filmmakers are just doing perfunctory work. They don't have any new ideas,' Kim complained.[2]

They agreed to Kim's suggestion to remarry and were promptly put to work for him. Notably, Choi tape-recorded a meeting with Kim, including one in which he apologised for the crude kidnappings. This daring move later helped the couple counter Kim's claim after they defected to Vienna in 1986 that Shin voluntarily came to North Korea after the South Korean government closed his studio.

After they defected to the United States, Shin and Choi remained together and moved to Los Angeles where Shin directed films under a pseudonym. They eventually returned to South Korea, where Shin died in 2006. Choi died in April 2018 at the age of ninety-one.

1 Gorenfeld, John. 'Kidnapped by Kim Jong-il: the Man Who Directed the Socialist Godzilla.' *The Guardian*, 4 Apr. 2003, http://bit.ly/2LuU1PC.
2 Secondary reference: Shin's book *Kingdom of Kim* is not available in English

60. KIM MADE SEVEN FILMS WITH HIS SOUTH KOREAN PRISONERS

Shin and Choi made seven films with Kim serving as executive producer. These three really stand out:

> *Runaway*, which Shin called his best film and won Best Director at the 1984 Prague Film Festival
>
> *Pulgasari*, a retelling of the Godzilla story
>
> *Salt*, which won Choi Best Actress at the 1985 Moscow Film Festival

Runaway (1984) is based on a short story that takes place during the Japanese occupation of Korea. It opens with a quote from *Les Miserables* and is about a peasant family torn apart when a wealthier relative sells the farm where they work to a Japanese businessman. The father is killed for protesting the sale and the family flees to the lawless Manchuria. Things go from bad to worse: the mother (played by Choi) is attacked by rabid dogs owned by ... a businessman.

After a local pharmacist refuses to sell medicine for less than full price, a son (the film's protagonist) loses it and sets fire to the pharmacy. He is sent to prison, and later freed by Kim Il-sung and his band of guerrillas (reminiscent of the account in Fact 4). He joins the guerrillas and in the film's climax, blows up a Japanese army train.

Shin jokingly asked for a real train to fill with explosives for this scene. He got it. The scene is considered an iconic one in North Korean cinema.

Salt (1985; *Sogum* in Korean) is a tragedy about a peasant woman in Manchuria (Choi) whose son has run off to fight with a guerrilla army. Also based on a novel about the occupation, *Salt* is heavy on socialist realism: the wealthy and landowners rape the poor, who are generous and struggle together.

Salt turned North Korean film on its head in three ways:

It opens with a Bible quote: 'You are the salt of the earth. But if the salt loses is saltiness, how can it be made salty again?' (Matthew 5:13) This is pretty amazing in a country where Christians are often persecuted

It verged on sexploitation, at least by the standards of the time, and particularly in North Korea. Choi's scenes included full-frontal breastfeeding and a reportedly realistic rape

It was well received by the foreign press.

Pulgasari (1985) is an iron-eating monster created from rice by an imprisoned blacksmith. At first, Pulgasari fights for the good of the people against an evil king. Then he turns against them and eats their tools. The blacksmith's daughter tells him he's gained too much weight and he shatters into pieces. Another Pulgasari emerges from the ocean.

The film was intended to be anti-capitalist; I guess both the king and the monster represent capitalism or its lure. The part where the monster gains too much weight is kind of prophetic. And it sure did echo what Kim Il-sung did to Korea. His son loved it anyway – until his star and director defected during an overseas trip to find a foreign distributor for it.

61. Kim Jong-il Had a Lot of Alcohol-related Health Problems

It's not too hard to see where Kim Jong-un inherited his expensive tastes. His father was said to be obsessed with alcohol, particularly Hennessy VSOP cognac. He spent more than $800,000 per year on it, making him one of its all-time leading buyers.

As early as the 1970s, Victor Cha writes, defectors who once served as his bodyguards reported Kim was an alcoholic and a chain-smoker with heart and liver complications.[1] He also liked wine. In 2000, a BBC profile reported he was seen 'draining 10 glasses of wine during a summit with South Korean President Kim Dae-jung'.[2]

By the1990s, there were rumours that Kim had diabetes and kidney disease. He suffered a stroke in August 2008 and disappeared from public view for several months. Outside news reports said he had heart bypass or brain surgery; the official North Korean media only acknowledged surgery. When he re-emerged, he looked gaunt and quite ill. A 2007 report in *The Guardian* notes that his hair was 'somewhat patchy in some places'.[3]

When former US president Bill Clinton met with Kim in 2009 to obtain the release of two US prisoners, he said Kim was energetic but showed classic stroke-related injuries: a limp and trembling on one side.

Cha relates an interesting story from a speech he gave to a convention of Korean-American spine and neurosurgeons. One of the attendees told him about an MRI he received from European colleagues that showed a cerebral haemorrhage.

---

1 Cha, *The Impossible State*, p. 94.

2 'Profile: Kim Jong-il.' *BBC News*, 16 Jan. 2009, https://bbc.in/2NqHTAH.

3 Walker, Peter. 'The Ailing Kim Jong-il?' *The Guardian*, 6 July 2007, http://bit.ly/2wrPzvj.

The (unnamed) patient wanted a second opinion from a Korean surgeon. The doctor told Cha he was certain it was Kim Jong-il's brain image.[4]

In 2016, North Korean defector Kim Hyeongsoo told a human rights conference in London about a scheme in which 130 scientists from the country's best universities were sent to Denmark allegedly to research beef. Kim Hyeongsoo, who was part of the group, learned their real mission was to find ways to promote Kim Jong-il's health and longevity. Some were told to develop aphrodisiacs, while others, oddly, were working to replicate his favourite Western cigarettes (Rothmans) with tobacco imported from Africa.[5]

Their laboratory, which was closely guarded with electric fences and armed personnel, also researched conditions and diseases Kim had a personal interest in (or experience of?): heart strength, diabetes, tuberculosis and sexual performance. Products were tested on humans (presumably North Koreans) and animals.

Cha says Kim wore large sunglasses because he had cataracts. He must have had them fixed because in 2006, he allowed a Nepalese eye surgeon, Sanduk Ruit, to bring a team into the country to train surgeons to perform cataract surgery.

---

4 Cha, p. 95.
5 Reuters. 'North Korea Defector Reveals Late Leader's Fears over Libido and Diabetes.' *Newsweek*, 28 May 2016, http://bit.ly/2BRBYDz.

62. KIM JONG-IL JUMPED OVER TWO OLDER SONS TO ANOINT KIM JONG-UN HIS HEIR

Kim Jong-un wasn't born to be Supreme Leader. Kim Jong-il intended his eldest son, Kim Jong-nam, to succeed him.

This ended when he was detained in Japan in 2000 travelling under a passport from the Dominican Republic as 'Pan Xiong,' with two women, a young boy, and lots of bling. Japanese immigration officials, alerted about a person of interest, questioned 'Pan'. As Victor Cha points out, how many Chinese-Dominicans are there? Pan initially told them the family was headed to Disneyland. After an hour of questioning, he admitted the passports were fake. 'I am Kim Jong-un's son,' he declared, and asked for a hamburger.[1]

This was not exactly the person of interest expected, but it sealed the deal to dump the First Grandson in the succession.

Next up was Kim Jong-chul, who was passed over because his father found him effeminate, according to Kenji Fujimoto, Kim Jong-il's gossipy sushi chef whose memoir was a best-seller in Japan (sadly, it's not available in English).

Leaks from South Korean intelligence say Kim Jong-chul personally arrested his uncle Jang Song-thaek, who was subsequently executed. Kim Jong-nam's fate is discussed in Fact 63.

The BBC and other news outlets reported seeing Kim Jong-chul at Eric Clapton concerts in Germany, Singapore, and London, 'having a great time, singing along to all the words'.[2]

1 Cha, *The Impossible State*, p. 97.
2 'Kim Jong-un's Brother Visits London to Watch Eric Clapton.' *BBC News*, 22 May 2015, https://bbc.in/2wvz6pW.

63. KIM JONG-UN HAD HIS OLDER HALF-BROTHER MURDERED

When Kim Jong-nam saw his youngest brother elevated to the rank of a four-star general, he realised he'd lost his place forever. In 2012, he went on an offensive, calling Kim Jong-un a joke, and predicted the new regime wouldn't last. In response, his funds were cut off and there was at least one assassination attempt on him. In 2012, he wrote to Kim Jong-un begging for himself and his family: 'We have nowhere to hide. The only way to escape is suicide.'[1]

On 13 February 2017, two women approached him in the Kuala Lumpur International Airport as he headed towards the Air Asia check-in. One after the other, they covered his eyes and smeared an oily substance over his face and mouth. The substance was VX, a potent lethal agent. Kim stumbled to an information desk gasping in English that he was in pain. He had a seizure, paramedics arrived, and he died fifteen minutes later on the way to hospital.

The two women – Siti Aisyah from Indonesia and Doan Thi Huong from Vietnam – were identified by security cameras and arrested the following morning. They did not know one another. It turns out both were recruited by North Korean agents and thought they were filming pranks for YouTube and Japanese television They were stunned to be accused of murder, punishable by death in Malaysia. As this goes to press, the trial is in recess.

---

1 Clark, Doug Bock, and Jesse Chehak. 'The Untold Story of Kim Jong-Nam's Assassination.' *GQ*, 25 Sept. 2017, http://bit.ly/2MZJUXW.

64. NORTH KOREA HAS ONE OF THE WORLD'S WORST HUMAN RIGHTS RECORDS

Human rights abuses is one area where North Korea is an undisputed leader.

A briefing paper released in June 2018 by Human Rights Watch says North Korea is one of the world's most repressive states and lists some of the routine offences that go on in the country:

Restricted civil and political liberties for citizens including no freedom of expression, no right to assembly, no right to form associations, and no right to religious practice

No independent media

Routine and arbitrary arrests

Torture of people in custody

Use of forced labour and executions to maintain fear and control

Punishment of citizens who make contact with the outside world.[1]

A United Nations Commission of Inquiry into North Korea's human rights abuses found additional violations, particularly against political prisoners:

Extermination
Murder
Enslavement
Rape
Forced abortion

---

1 'Human Rights in North Korea.' *Human Rights Watch*, 5 June 2018, http://bit.ly/2MTO9UQ.

There have also been reports of infanticide in prisons.[2]

Incredibly, North Korea has signed numerous human rights treaties that expressly prohibit these crimes. Lesser (as in usually non-fatal) human rights abuses include not protecting vulnerable groups such as children, people with disabilities, prisoners, and women, who are subject to gender-based punishments. For example, married women can be punished for their husbands' crimes, and women and girls in prison are often raped and sexually violated in other ways.

Women do not hold any senior positions in the Workers' Party, the only political party permitted to operate in North Korea. (Membership is also more difficult for women to attain.) Women are also poorly represented in government positions, making up only 17 per cent of officials in the Ministry of Foreign Affairs and 5 per cent of diplomats. Just 12 per cent of judges and lawyers are women, and 10 per cent of divisional directors.[2]

North Koreans face arrest for reasons that are difficult for outsiders to comprehend:

Failing to properly display required framed portraits of the Great Leader and Dear Leader in the home

Falling asleep during official meetings; Kim Jong-un executed a general for this reason

Displaying 'disrespectful posture,' which got the deputy premier for education executed

Defecting: North Koreans 'repatriated' by China and other nations are immediately imprisoned upon their return

Foreigners are also subject to arrest. The American student Otto Warmbier confessed to stealing a propaganda poster

2 International Bar Association. *North Korea: Inquiry Finds Kim Jong-un Should Be Investigated and Prosecuted for Crimes against Humanity*, http://bit.ly/2wrQCeJ.

from a staff-only area in the hotel he was staying in with a tour group. He was sentenced to fifteen years in prison and freed seventeen months later after he fell into a coma. He died six days after returning to the US No explanation has been found for his condition; there were no signs of torture, nor the botulism North Korea claims he contacted.

Other foreigners have been arrested and charged with spying, 'hostile acts' against the state – religious practitioners are often charged with this – and illegally entering the country.

65. THERE ARE FOUR KINDS OF PRISON IN NORTH KOREA

There are four unique kinds of North Korean prisons: detention centres, labour camps, re-education and labour camps, and concentration camps.

Detention centres, or jibkyulso, are operated by the People's Safety Agency police unit for people who commit minor violations, such as skipping out from work. They can also be sent to a rodong danryeondae, or labour camp, to work on road repair.

Kyohwaso are re-education and labour camps for prisoners convicted of more serious crimes, such as attempting to defect, or who commit economic crimes, like smuggling. While there, they are subjected to forced labour, which can include factory work, equipment repair, or just chopping wood. They attend ideology and self-criticism sessions and sleep on bare floors with thin blankets to cover them, which provide little protection against North Korean winters that have temperatures as low as -20°C (-4°F). Food is poor, with little rice (a Korean staple) or protein. It is not unusual for prisoners to starve to death; many who survive are severely malnourished. There are accounts of families bribing security officials to release members from kyohwaso camps.

If this doesn't sound horrifying enough, the worst fates await political prisoners and Christians, who are put in kwanliso, camps that are, frankly, gulags or concentration camps. In December 2017, The International Bar Association (IBA) War Crimes Committee released a report on these camps, which they concluded are guilty of ten of the eleven crimes against humanity outlawed by the International Criminal Court (ICC).[1]

---

1 International Bar Association, www.ibanet.org/Article/NewDetail. aspx?ArticleUid=8ae0f29d-4283-4151-a573-a66b2c1ab480

The ICC's Thomas Buergenthal, who worked on the report, is a child survivor of Kielce, a Polish ghetto for Jews, and the Sachsenhausen and Auschwitz concentration camps. He told *The Washington Post* that the North Korean gulags are 'as terrible, or even worse, than those I saw and experienced in my youth in these Nazi camps and in my long professional career in the human rights field'.[2]

The IBA *Inquiry on Crimes Against Humanity in North Korean Political Prisons* report debunks North Korea's claim that such camps do not exist. In addition to horrifying and consistent details provided by a few survivors and a prison guard who escaped the country, satellite images have identified where many of these camps are.

The crimes reported are truly horrifying, worse than any horror film; I can only describe them as medieval and worse. I wouldn't recommend reading the report unless you have a strong stomach for details of deprivation, which go beyond these 'routine' human rights violations:

Murder
Extermination
Enslavement
Torture
Sexual violence
Persecution, in this case against Christians

Children are not spared, either. Each year, these camps deliberately overwork and starve as many as 2,000 prisoners – mostly children. Many are there because of a family member's alleged crime, sometimes committed long before they were born.[1]

---

2 Fifield, Anna. 'North Korea's Prisons Are as Bad as Nazi Camps, Says Judge Who Survived Auschwitz.' *The Washington Post*, 11 Dec. 2017.

66. Around 1 Per Cent of All North Koreans Are in Prison, Including Descendants of Earlier Prisoners

Back in 2013, a human rights specialist named Barbara Cohen was serving as a senior fellow at the Brookings Institution, a Washington DC think tank. Cohen, now with Georgetown University's School of Foreign Service, delivered a talk in which she estimated that North Korea had 100,000–200,000 of its people in prison camps.[1] This includes whole families who are imprisoned together.

That amounted to around 1 per cent of the population. (The US has no *numerical* bragging rights, at around 0.7 per cent.) Recent estimates are near the high end of Cohen's estimate and include prisoners in re-education (kyohwaso) camps. Victor Cha says the number is 200,000–300,000, and that around 1 million prisoners have died in North Korea's gulags.[2]

Family imprisonment is the result of Kim Il-sung's 1972 edict that punishes up to three generations of some prisoners' descendants, intended to 'wipe out the "seed" of class enemies', as *The Economist* explains.[3] Family members are often arrested and imprisoned when a member defects to another nation (usually South Korea) or commits a political crime. They are charged with having 'wrong thoughts'; in other words, they are guilty by blood association.

The International Bar Association estimates that 1,500–2,000 children starve to death in North Korean prisons each year.[4]

---

1 Cohen, Barbara. 'Time to Address North Korea's Prison Labor Camps.' The Asian Institute for Policy Studies, 4 July 2013.
2 Cha, *The Impossible State*, p.172.
3 International Bar Association, http://bit.ly/2wrQCeJ.
4 'The Gulag behind the Goose-Steps.' *The Economist*, 21 Apr. 2012, https://econ.st/2NqIAdh.

67. Thousands of North Koreans Have Defected to Other Countries

Thousands of North Koreans have defected since the DMZ was established in 1953. Total numbers are difficult to come by and are even harder to substantiate since many defectors are unable to become legal citizens of the countries they escape to.

Historically, North Koreans defect to China and the Soviet Union/Russia, countries that share its borders. Unlike the smaller number of defectors who make it to South Korea, they live underground and don't dare to publicly announce their presence lest they be deported back to North Korea and almost certain death in a camp for political prisoners. At one point several thousand North Koreans, of whom many had escaped prison camps, lived in the Russian Far East but the Russian border no longer appears to be a viable destination.

South Korea's Unification Ministry says the country has absorbed around 31,000 defectors from the north; about 71 per cent are women. Getting to South Korea is an arduous process that involves finding a human trafficker, or broker, who will help them cross into China from the northern border with Liaoning province. Then they must get through Vietnam and Laos, or Myanmar, and into Thailand. They can be repatriated at every step until they reach Thailand, although Vietnam has co-operated with South Korea in recent years thanks to that country's investment in its economy.

Once in Thailand, refugees are usually arrested on immigration violations. After a brief stay in a detention centre, they are turned over to the South Korean Embassy in Bangkok. That starts the process of entering South Korea.

Others go through Mongolia, which won't repatriate North Korean refugees and sends them directly to South Korea. However, the Chinese-Mongolian border is pretty tight and getting there requires going through the Gobi Desert – not a day at the beach.

Many defectors remain in China, especially women. Thanks to China's former one-child policy that led to countless deaths of female infants and abortions of female foetuses, there is a serious shortage of eligible women to marry, particularly in rural areas. North Korean women, who generally arrive with little or no money, rarely have the money to pay for the long trip to South Korea. They are sold by traffickers to brokers who in turn sell them to rural families looking for wives. Many find themselves in pretty awful circumstances that include hours of hard labour and bad treatment. You can read more about Korean wives in the next Fact, 68.

Some women are treated reasonably well and are allowed to work and earn some money. Yeonmi Park knew a woman who worked for an adult chat room and eventually saved enough money to open her own chat business. Others, like Park, become partners to 'brokers' and provide a bizarre kind of orientation to newly arrived North Korean women about their probable futures.

North Koreans in elite positions who are permitted to travel to the West have defected at embassies that include EU nations, Canada and the United States.

68. Many North Korean Women Who Escape to China Live Underground as 'Wives' to Chinese Men

China's one-child policy that lasted from 1979 to 2016 created a serious shortage of women in the country. This created something of an opportunity for North Korean women looking to escape and certainly increased opportunities for human smuggling/trafficking.

Many North Korean women who escape to China are aware that they will probably be sold as a wife, which they obviously consider a better deal than remaining in North Korea. Those who don't know what to expect are usually younger or simply less savvy. They may be lured over the border with promises of good jobs by smugglers looking to provide wives to Chinese men. Ironically, women who share their plans to leave are usually better prepared. There is a substantial underground industry to match smugglers with illegal émigrés and prepare them for the journey into China and its aftermath.

Of course, these marriages aren't legal since China does not accept North Korean refugees and has actively hunted them down. Many of the 'marriages' are to poor farmers in the rural border regions, say authors Yeonmi Park and Lucia Jang, who both escaped to China before eventually reaching friendly nations that sent them to South Korea.

Park's mother was sold to a Chinese man and did hard labour on a farm. Park became an unwilling concubine and business partner to the broker who 'bought' them but ultimately earned enough money to buy her mother back.

Several potential husbands rejected Jang because she didn't speak Chinese. She was finally sold to be a companion, so to speak, to a man with low intelligence. She fled the situation and much to the amazement of her traffickers, returned to ask for another placement. She was then sold to a farm family to provide labour and eventually moved in with one of the younger brothers. I won't give away the rest of her story, but it's an amazing one that includes not one, but two stints in North Korean prisons for illegally leaving the country.

Living in China means living underground. There is no such thing as a North Korean refugee. Women living illegally in China can't travel safely or socialise too much. They may be abused by their 'husbands' and family members. There doesn't appear to be any punishment for families caught with illegal North Koreans since they can always claim they were unaware of their status.

Even today, with famine always looming, China looks like a better bet to many North Korean women, who often grow up with ingrained sexism and violence. They have a more difficult time getting into university than men, or joining the dominant Korean Workers' Party, a necessity to advance to get better jobs, housing, and food allocations. If they marry, and most do, they can be punished for crimes committed by husbands or other relatives. Living underground may not look so bad from the other side of the border.

69. Many Neighbouring Countries Return North Korean Refugees

North Korea has diplomatic and at times, trade relationships with its neighbours. For that reason, many of them will return, or 'repatriate,' people who defect. China has even allowed North Korean agents to cross the border to hunt down defectors.

This is particularly cruel since in the past, China didn't interfere with North Korean refugees attempting to reach foreign embassies or consulates. Reaching one, though, is difficult: the border region is a cold one, although that allows escapees to cross the iced-over Yalu River, which makes up the entire 790-km (491-mile) border. Things may be changing; there are reports that China is constructing refugee camps along the border with Jilin province, where the narrow Tumen River is a well-known escape point.

China is a signatory to the 1951 United Nations Convention on Refugees, which stipulates that refugees cannot be returned to their home countries if this puts them at risk of persecution or torture. Its repeated violation of this convention has been raised numerous times in the UN Security Council (where China is a permanent member along with the UK, US, Russia, and France). The US signed the 1967 Protocol that widened the convention's scope; all other Security Council members signed both versions.

Russia signed an agreement with North Korea in 2014 that stipulates the two countries will forcibly repatriate anyone found residing illegally within their borders. The two countries share a tiny, 17-km (11-mile) land and 22-km (12-nautical mile) border. Researchers with the Henry Jackson Society believe there are only around forty North Koreans hiding out in Russia.

Between 2004 and 2017, Russia granted asylum to just three North Korean defectors. One was Choe Myong-bok, who was scheduled to be forcibly deported after he voluntarily answered a police summons supposedly about his application for refugee status. Choe was spared repatriation after a court dismissed the case against him. This had to be a huge relief; an earlier North Korean refugee who was forcibly repatriated in 2008 was executed in a particularly gruesome style: lashed to a moving train and dragged to death. Choe has since re-applied for asylum.

Former North Korean prisoners have testified about torture they endured upon repatriation, most recently in December 2017. 'Not many people made it alive out of this place [a North Korean prison for defectors],' one woman testified, adding that her physical injuries will never fully heal.[1] Not surprisingly, Russia and China always vote against hearing such testimony.

David Hawk, a former executive director of Amnesty International, says the Chinese also make regular sweeps of border towns inside Jilin and neighbouring province Liaoning to hunt and capture women who've escaped North Korea.[1] Lucia Jang and Yeonmi Park, who have both written books about their escapes from North Korea, back this up in their accounts.

---

1 'UN Meeting Calls for China to Stop Sending North Korean Defectors Home.' *South China Morning Post*, 12 Dec. 2017, http://bit.ly/2wrousm.

70. North Korea Has Regularly Kidnapped Citizens of Japan and South Korea

North Korea has kidnapped foreigners almost since its founding. Kim Il-sung announced a plan in 1946 to 'transport' half a million people from the South to the North, particularly intellectuals. Around 84,000 South Koreans were kidnapped during the Korean War, according to an article by Robert Boynton for *The New Yorker*.[1]

It's thought that as many as 3,800 people have been kidnapped since the 1953 armistice, mostly from Japan and South Korea. The late 1970s was more or less the heyday of kidnappings, when an unusual number of Japanese citizens began vanishing from their own country in 1977. Some were young, still in their teens. Kidnapping victims who have escaped report that they were used to educate spies about their countries so that they can blend into these nations. This 'service' would help unite the peninsula.

Young couples were considered particularly attractive to kidnap with the hope that they would have children who would grow up to be loyal to the Juche nation. Couples were sometimes separated and later reunited to marry.

Charles Jenkins, an American serviceman who defected to North Korea and left for Japan (see Fact 21), told Boynton that he believed the kidnappings were part of a 'seed-bearing scheme' to produce mixed-raced children who can blend in, in various places, as spies. He believes his own children (his wife herself was abducted from Japan) were being pushed to become spies. This was instrumental in their decision to request asylum in Japan during a state-approved visit.

Women from the Middle East and Eastern Europe were lured to North Korea with the promise of jobs. Many

---

1   Boynton, Robert S. 'North Korea's Abduction Project.' *The New Yorker*, 1 Sept. 2017, http://bit.ly/2ogcGFI.

ended up in arranged, if not forced, marriages. Some were wed in a mass ceremony in 1977 to so-called Red Army members, young Japanese men with Communist sentiments who had hijacked an airliner to North Korea in 1970. The scheme came to be known as The Marriage Project, which certainly lends credence to Jenkins' suspicions. Furthermore, Kim Il-sung told the newlyweds that their children would continue the revolution into the next generation.

The outside world didn't piece together these disappearances until 1987, when two North Korean terrorists confessed to bombing a South Korean airliner. One said she was taught Japanese by an instructor who had been kidnapped.

In 2002, Kim Jong-il met with Japanese Prime Minister Junichiro Koizumi at the DMZ to discuss missing people. Koizumi demanded an apology for the disappearances. After a short break, Kim read a statement in which he apologised for 'regrettable conduct' of blindly motivated commandos behind hundreds, if not thousands, of abductions. He also said the people responsible for the highly publicised kidnapping of thirteen-year-old Megumi Yokota in 1977 had been punished: one by execution, one with a fifteen-year prison sentence. To this day, no one is certain if Yokota is dead, as North Korea says, or is living there under a different name.

71. THE NORTH KOREAN GOVERNMENT OUTSOURCES ITS PEOPLE TO OTHER NATIONS FOR CHEAP LABOUR

North Koreans with higher songbun classifications are often selected to work in other nations to provide cheap labour. Their pay amounts to around £15 ($20) per month after the North Korean government takes its cut, which may be as much as £1.5 billion ($2 billion) per year according to a report from *The Washington Post*.[1]

Around 60,000 labourers work in around twenty countries in dangerous industries such as logging, mining, and construction, mostly in China and Russia, where they built at least one stadium for the 2018 World Cup. They also work in Middle Eastern and African nations. In addition to poor pay, they are sometimes forced to work twelve–twenty-hour days, with one or two days off per month, *The Guardian* reports.[2]

Poland stopped providing work visas to North Korean workers in 2016 in response to sanctions for nuclear test ban treaty violations, and Kuwait and Qatar expelled its North Korean workers. Russia and China, who were reluctant to give up cheap labour, got the UN to agree to let them keep workers until the end of their contracts, which generally last three to five years.

Some workers take the opportunity to defect, but this isn't easy given the long working hours and near-constant surveillance. Plus, most of the workers selected for overseas labour are married with families who they know may

---

1 Aldag, Jason. 'How North Korea Takes a Cut from Its Workers Abroad.' *The Washington Post*, 1 Nov. 2017, https://wapo.st/2of60Yp.

2 Associated Press. 'North Korea Putting Thousands into Forced Labour Abroad, UN Says.' *The Guardian*, 29 Oct. 2015, http://bit.ly/2oePOWQ.

be subject to harassment, job or housing loss, or even imprisonment should they defect. And even though they are selected for their good songbun status and family ties, they are still put into a reintegration plan and are under strict surveillance for three years when they return to North Korea. This is because they've no doubt seen some of the freedoms enjoyed by others outside the country, according to Jae H. Ku, who directed the now defunct US-Korea Institute at Johns Hopkins University.[1] (The institute lost its major funding source, the South Korean government, in April 2018.)

Kim Seung-chul was one labourer who defected after working in Siberia for two years. A graduate from a North Korean engineering university, he now runs a radio service, North Korea Reform Radio, in Seoul. He broadcasts programmes that target high-level officials in North Korea; almost all North Korean families with some standing have a secret radio or television tuned to receive broadcasts from the outside world. Kim shared intelligence with *The Washington Post* that includes a ledger tracking workers' earnings and performance goals. Some were falling behind and, according to a note in the ledger, would be fined: 'Workers pay attention only when you talk about their money.'[1] It seems that even those in the better songbun aren't quite so devoted to the Supreme Leader.

72. SOUTH KOREA MAY HAVE KIDNAPPED NORTH KOREANS WORKING IN CHINA

In April 2016, the South Korean government announced that twelve waitresses in their twenties and thirties, who had been working in a government-run restaurant, had defected with their manager.

They were among thousands of North Korean nationals sent to work in China, Russia, the Middle East and various African nations, in order to provide badly needed hard currency to North Korea. Many work in restaurants and factories, while others are in fairly dangerous occupations such as logging and construction.

Two years later, in May 2018, the same manager told a South Korean news show that he worked with South Korea's National Intelligence Service to 'lure and kidnap' the women.[1] Three of them appeared with him and asked to go home. 'I miss my parents,' one said.

Here are some red flags (to use an ironic term) around the defection story:

The group arrived in South Korea just two days after they disappeared from their jobs. Normally, it takes months to reach South Korea from where they were, in the city of Ningbo in Zhejiang Province. The journey usually requires going through jungles and negotiating with human traffickers.

The government announced the group defection – the largest ever in the country's history – the day after the refugees arrived.

1 Choe, Sang-hun. 'Tale of North Korean Waitresses Who Fled to South Takes Dark Turn.' *The New York Times*, 11 May 2018, https://nyti.ms/2MW4Ej3.

The women interviewed said they only knew they were going to work at a different place. They were flown to Malaysia and were shocked to find themselves taken to the South Korean Embassy in Kuala Lumpur. At least some balked at entering it.

Finally, this scheme came about under President Park Geun-hye, who was impeached and removed from office in 2017 and charged with bribery, abuse of power, and corruption. She is currently serving a 24-year prison sentence.

The manager, Heo Kang-il, was apparently angered by Kim Jong-il's execution of five of his former classmates caught up in a purge of officials close to Kim's uncle, Jang Song-thaek, who was himself executed in 2013 for treason, corruption, sedition, etc. Heo said he met with a South Korean agent in 2014 and pledged his allegiance to the spy agency. Two years later, he was on the brink of exposure and asked his contact to help him defect. Because the operation was approved by then-President Park, Heo said, he had to take the women with him or he would be reported to the North Korean Embassy.

Heo in turn blackmailed the waitresses by threatening to report they often watched South Korean movies. 'If you return home, you die, and if you follow me, you live. I am now remorseful for what I did.' The women, who said they loved their jobs in China, really had no choice. Families of North Korean prisoners are often charged with crimes as well, and sentences often last for generations, as discussed in Fact 66.

73. Some Defectors Return to North Korea

As many as 25 per cent of North Korean defectors to the South seriously consider returning, Australia's *ABC News* reports.[1] Going back, or double defecting, is illegal in South Korea, which says thirteen defectors have returned. It's probably a lot higher: ABC reports that the whereabouts of around 800 others known to have entered South Korea are unknown.

South Korea is not an easy place for North Koreans. They suffer around six times the national average from depression and unemployment, according to ABC. Many North Korean defectors become socially isolated and are actively discriminated against by their new compatriots; South Koreans can be pretty snobby. '[We] defectors are forever strangers in this country, classified as second class citizens ... treated like cigarette ashes thrown away on the streets,' one woman told *The Guardian*. 'I would never want my daughter to live this life.'[2]

But it's not as if the South Korean government doesn't try to ease the transition. After they have satisfied the National Intelligence Service that they are not spies (a time frame that was reduced in 2018 from a maximum of 180 days to ninety), defectors enter one of two support facilities where they live for three months and are educated about living in South Korea: social norms, the actual history of the two Koreas, and how to use technology like ATM cards.

Once they graduate from the facility, defectors receive a resettlement package from the government that includes a

---

1 Carney, Matthew. 'He Risked His Life to Escape North Korea. Now He Wants to Go Back.' *ABC News*, 15 Dec. 2017, https://ab.co/2wiNySP.

2 Haas, Benjamin. '"Forever Strangers"': the North Korean Defectors Who Want to Go Back.' *The Guardian*, 26 Apr. 2018, http://bit.ly/2MyXYYF.

very modest stipend paid over five years, subsidised housing, and job search assistance. If they decide to enrol in higher education, the government pays half the tuition.

Of course it isn't easy. Everything is new and it's understandable to feel horribly lonely. Even people who have made good lives in South Korea say they miss the camaraderie they felt in North Korea, where almost everyone was struggling together.

Guilt is another issue. Families of defectors often face job loss, being turned out of their homes, and even imprisonment. In recent years, though, Kim Jong-un has launched campaigns appealing to defectors to come back home, with promises of money, a job, and a home, just like in the good old pre-Arduous March days. 'In the DPRK,' one depressed ex-North Korean told ABC, 'it's one man and one rule and our great leader has said he will forgive people who have defected.' In 2018, Radio Free Asia reported that North Korea's state security has also ordered families of some defectors to call and convince them to return.

Defectors who return to North Korea are typically used for propaganda. They go on television to claim they were abducted and forced into a living hell. As promised, those who perform well are treated quite generously.

74. North Korea Does Not Report Its Gross Domestic Product

It's impossible to know North Korea's gross domestic product (GDP) because the country stopped reporting details in the 1960s. (GDP is the value, usually based on US dollars, of all finished goods and services produced inside a country.) Anything about North Korea's GDP is guesswork based on limited budget and health data the government releases, interviews with knowledgeable defectors, and good old spying, mostly by South Korea. Here is what North Korea reported for its spending in key areas between 2017 and 2018:

Science and technology, up 7.3 per cent

Public health, up 6 per cent

Education, up 6 per cent

Overall national economy (power, metal, chemicals, light industry, agriculture), up 5.5 per cent

Sports, up 5 per cent

'Improving economic independence', up 5 per cent

Forest restoration, up 5 per cent

Literature and art, up 3 per cent

Statistics are from Bloomberg, which explains that 'improving economic independence is defined as "Strengthening the independence and Juche character of the national economy and improving the standard of people's living".'[1] As a rule, North Korea only reports changes by percentages, not actual amounts, according to Marcus Noland, an economist and

---

1 McIntyre, Alex, and Adrian Leung. 'How Big Is North Korea's Economy? Pick a Number, Any Number.' Bloomberg.com, 10 June 2018, https://bloom.bg/2PbiDyX.

political observer with the Peterson Institute for International Economics in Washington DC[2] Actual numbers are a closely guarded state secret.

South Korea, which pays more attention to North Korea than anyone, concludes that the North Korean economy is almost twice the size of official United Nations estimates. But as Noland wrote in the journal *Foreign Policy* in 2012, South Korea doesn't include its own investment and trade with North Korea because it considers it to be part of its territory. When you consider that South Korea is the eleventh-largest economy in the world, this is a considerable 'but' to factor in.[2]

In addition, trade numbers are difficult to confirm. There's good reason to suspect that nations that publicly condemn North Korea's missile testing and participate in sanctions allow back-door trading and investment to go on. They aren't going to report this. Some, Bloomberg says, confuse the two Koreas but who's to say this isn't a deliberate muddle? After all, who wants to be the target of a Trump tweet, even for a day?

Noland says he's only 'half-joking' when he says he makes up half his North Korea data. Many sources, he wrote, are 'half-serious' in that they use data such as UN infant mortality statistics and crop data to estimate per capita income. But they aren't enough to provide accurate yearly estimates for GDP In all likelihood, no one except a handful of top North Korean officials really know the truth about the economy.[2] Given their historically precarious lifespans, that number can easily shrink and make the circle of people who know these state secrets even smaller.

2   Noland, Marcus. 'The Black Hole of North Korea.' *Foreign Policy*, 7 Mar. 2012, http://bit.ly/2MQY1i4.

75. SOUTH KOREA OPERATED A JOINT INDUSTRIAL DISTRICT WITH NORTH KOREA

In 2002, the two Koreas established a joint economic zone in the North Korean city of Kaesong, around 10 kilometres (6 miles) north of the DMZ, around an hour's drive from Seoul.

Both nations benefitted from the arrangement: South Korea had access to inexpensive labour and untapped mineral resources, while the North Korean government received around 70 per cent of the £77 million ($100 million) in wages and profits generated by its workers.[1] One-hundred-and-twenty-four companies were operating in 2016, including electronics firms, clothing and textile manufacturing, light industry, and chemical products, making it a pretty well-rounded economic powerhouse.

Although it's a business enterprise, Kaesong operations are dependent on goodwill between both nations and particularly North Korean attitudes toward treaties and other agreements. The complex has twice been closed because of political tensions. The first time was in April 2013, when North Korea blocked access to the region after it (1) pulled out of the 1953 armistice agreement, (2) launched a cyber attack against the South, (3) severed the North-South hotline, (4) declared a state of war with the South, and (5) announced it would restart plutonium production.

At the time, around 800 South Koreans and 53,000 North Koreans worked in Kaesong; expelling the South's workers effectively shut down the entire complex. All was forgiven a few months later, in August 2013, when both countries announced the complex would reopen and business was back to 'Make Korea Great Again!'

---

1 Padden, Brian. 'Kaesong Business Owners Anxious for N. Korea Sanctions to End.' Voice of America, 28 June 2018, http://bit. ly/2PcUAQd.

But in early 2016, the North began testing missiles and a nuclear bomb, and South Korea promptly recalled all 280 workers from Kaesong and froze all its assets and equipment there. Since then, Kaesong's business and factory owners (all from South Korea) have not been able to visit the complex, which will only reopen when UN sanctions are lifted. Moon Jae-in, who took office in May 2017, will not allow the complex to reopen if North Korea continues to refuse to allow UN observers to visit and verify that nuclear test sites have been closed.

Kaesong's limited operations were pretty much halted in September 2017 when the UN imposed additional sanctions that blocked financial investments from other nations into non-military Kaesong operations such as its clothing and textile factories. A month later, one of the North's propaganda offices claimed the Kaesong factories were still producing clothing. 'The dogs may bark, but the caravan goes on.'[2]

Research and development is permitted, however, and President Moon reportedly gave Kim a thumb drive with details about a $35 billion railroad infrastructure plan for the two nations when they met in May 2018. In August 2018, Moon released a statement allowing the inter-Korean liaison office to continue its work in Kaesong.

---

2 'North Korea Says It Is Operating Kaesong Factories, "Freezes" Assets Valued at $663 Million Left by Seoul.' *The Japan Times*, http://bit.ly/2vTcpww.

76. NORTH KOREA'S CONSTITUTION PROTECTS RELIGIOUS FREEDOM

I know what you're thinking: 'yeah, right.'

I was just as surprised to read that the North Korean constitution guarantees freedom of religion but there it is, in Article 68 of Chapter V – *Fundamental Rights and Duties of Citizens*:

> Citizens have freedom of religious beliefs. This right is granted by approving the construction of religious buildings and the holding of religious ceremonies.

Religion, however, cannot be used as a 'pretext for drawing in foreign forces or harming the state or social order'. Furthermore, Article 66 declares the rights of citizens who have reached age seventeen to elect and be elected irrespective of 'sex, race, occupation, length of residence, property status, education party affiliation, political views or religion'.[1]

So why can't you bring a Bible or Koran into the country? Well, actually, you can if you are part of a faith-based aid organisation, according to the US State Department report on religious freedom in North Korea. What you can't do is give it away or do a public reading or otherwise engage in evangelical activities, which include even casual conversation or education.

The reason has to do with Juche, the official 'religion' in North Korea. Juche proclaims that whichever Kim is in power is the Supreme Leader. Refusing to accept this because of a belief that God, Jesus, Buddha, Mohammed, Krishna, or other deity or otherwise revered figure is in any

---

1 'Chapter V, Fundamental Rights and Duties of Citizens.' *KFAUSA. org*, http://bit.ly/2MQdfnz.

way superior to Kim is a direct challenge to the state and social order. Should someone proclaim himself of herself to be an adherent of a religion, there will be repercussions, starting with loss of status. Christians, in particular, are relegated to the lowest part of the songbun, which will pass down to their descendants as well.

South Korea's Institute for National Unification released a white paper on human rights in North Korea where it noted that there are state-sanctioned religious organisations for Christians, Catholics, Buddhists, Orthodox (Russian) Church, Cheondists, and 'Religionists'. Cheondoism, or Heavenly Way, is a twentieth-century movement that blends Confucian, Buddhist, and Taoist thought with Korean shamanism. The Oxford Dictionary defines religionism as 'excessive religious zeal'. Perhaps the Religionists in North Korea are excessive Juche devotees.

The Database Center for North Korean Human Rights, another organisation in South Korea, says there are around 120 religious facilities in the North, including sixty-four Buddhist temples, fifty-two Cheondist temples, and five Christian churches. Most North Koreans appear unaware that the Buddhist temples once had a religious significance; many see them in cultural and historical terms. The 1,000-year-old Proyoung Temple, a national treasure supported by the state, is run by twenty monks who conduct Buddhist ceremonies for visitors.

Journalist Suki Kim, undercover as an evangelical English instructor at the church-built Pyongyang University for Science and Technology, describes a church she was taken to for a Sunday service that she was convinced was entirely fake, right down to the supposed parishioners.

77. ONE OF NORTH KOREA'S ELITE UNIVERSITIES IS RUN BY EVANGELICAL CHRISTIANS

North Korea's government will accept aid from Christians as long as they don't proselytise. Nowhere is this more evident than in the Pyongyang University of Science and Technology (PUST, https://pust.co), the only private university in North Korea and one of its top three institutions.

PUST opened in 2010 and is modelled on China's Yanbian University of Science and Technology (YUST). Both schools were founded by Dr Kim Chin-kyung, who also goes by the name James Kim, in 1992. Born in Seoul, he was educated in England and the US, where he ran a business and earned an economics degree. During a trip to North Korea in 1998 to help with food aid, Kim, himself an evangelical Christian, was arrested and imprisoned on charges of spying. He was released after forty days. Three years later, North Korean authorities approached him to ask if he would create another YUST in Pyongyang.

Most of PUST's funding comes from evangelical Christian groups and the South Korean Ministry of Unification. All materials used to build and equip it came from China, Kim told *Fortune* in 2009. 'I have never brought any cash into North Korea.'[1]

American journalist Suki Kim, who spent a year teaching English at PUST, wrote that many of her students were from elite families. None went home during the summer break; they either remained on campus or worked on a collective farm.

The PUST faculty is unpaid. Kim's colleagues were all evangelical; to get the assignment, she pretended to share their faith. They were not permitted to discuss religion or their

---

1   Powell, Bill. 'The Capitalist Who Loves North Korea.' *Fortune*, 14 Sept. 2009, https://for.tn/2PbTa8v.

religious activities or beliefs with students. They attended a government-approved church, built with donations from South Korea. At one service, the pastor's sermon addressed the evils of the South Korean regime and its American Imperialist backers. It may have been a fake church; after the service, Kim noticed the 'parishioners' quickly walking away 'as though they had dispensed with their morning duty'.[2]

In 2017, two current and former PUST instructors holding US passports were arrested and jailed. Kim Sang-duk, who goes by the English name Tony, was arrested at Pyongyang Airport in April of that year after teaching a month-long class in international finance and management. A month later, Kim Hak-song was arrested for engaging in 'hostile acts' while doing development work at the school's farm. Both men were released in May 2018, along with a third American man arrested in 2015, just before US President Donald Trump met with Kim Jong-un.

PUST has separate colleges for business, engineering, and agriculture as well as a School of Foreign Languages that grant undergraduate degrees. Graduate degrees are also offered in engineering, business, agriculture, and life sciences. A Medical Sciences Division is under construction that will offer degrees in medicine, dentistry, pharmacy, nursing, and public health.

2 Kim, *Without You There Is No Us*, p. 139.

78. NORTH KOREAN PRIMARY SCHOOLS EXIST TO REINFORCE THE KIMS' RULE AND ARE NOT FREE

Education in North Korea exists to reinforce the Kims' rule as much as to teach basic skills. They are also not entirely free: students or their families must pay for things such as desks, chairs, heat, and uniforms. Some schools also expect students to take food and gifts to teachers. Those who can't afford all this pay off their bills by working for the state doing things such as collecting scrap material or cutting down trees, even when they are supposed to be in school. In some places, students spend half of their school days working off their tuition.

Children from better-off songbun families do not have to worry about paying for these items. Their schools are also far more attractive and comfortable and have modern tools like computers and projection screens. But even they are expected to spend time during school holidays to work for the good of the nation at farms, construction sites, and other places where physical labour is required. In 2017, high school and college classes were delayed until 11 a.m. so that students could help with watering crops in the early morning hours at local farms during a drought.

Children who live in labour camps as a result of the practice that punishes three generations for political crimes do not go to school at all. They provide hard labour to the state. If they survive to puberty things get worse: guards rape, abuse, and torture child prisoners, even to death.

North Korean schools spend a lot of time propagating the Juche system and Kim cult. Portraits of the two deceased Kims are in every classroom and hallway. Each school day begins with students and teachers bowing to them and pledging loyalty to the 'eternal leaders'.

Young children are taught songs about the Kims. Textbooks are filled with stories about their uncanny abilities, such as controlling the weather (Kim Il-sung) to learning to drive at age three (Kim Jong-un) to recording an under-par score at his first-ever golf outing (Kim Jong-il). History lessons focus on Korean enslavement by the Japanese and landlords' abuse of peasants before Kim Il-sung saved the nation. Anti-American messages are central; kindergarteners are taught 'drills' where they throw toy grenades and aim toy rifles at cartoonish images of Yankee invaders. Sometimes, children denounce specific enemies or criminals and may be required to watch public executions.

There are mandatory trips to Kim memorials, particularly after children are old enough to enrol in the Children's Union. Many are drafted to learn card-flipping skills for rallies where they and thousands of others create enormous mosaics of one or more of the Kims or other propaganda images.

The better schools identify students at a young age who show special talents in art and music and send them for intensive instruction. Creativity, however, is strictly curtailed to a curriculum that makes every work of art – dance, music, etc. – an homage to the Kims.

79. Kim Jong-un Attended Foreign Schools in Switzerland

Depending on the source you read, Kim Jong-un attended one or two different primary schools in Switzerland at various times during the 1990s. He apparently did attend a private school, possibly the International School of Bern, where he enrolled under an assumed name and was known as a diplomat's son, or sometimes as the son of the North Korean ambassador to Switzerland. It's also been reported that he attended a state-run school near Bern starting in 1991 or 1992. No schools have confirmed his attendance, or that of 'Pak Un', the name he was given to use.

People who are certain they were classmates of Kim's remember him as interested in sports, particularly basketball, and that he was a good player in spite of being slightly overweight. He was friendly, good for a laugh, loved to talk about sports, enjoyed video games, and wore expensive Nike trainers. A man who is certain 'Un' was one of his students told a news programme that he was a good but not extraordinary student – he needed additional tutoring in English and German – and had a good sense of humour. Because his older brother Kim Jong-chul also attended schools in and around Bern under pseudonyms (as did their sister Kim Yo-jong), it's possible that the two boys have been mixed up in people's memories.

The siblings lived a very normal life in Switzerland with their maternal aunt, her husband and their three children, in a house where, his aunt told *The Washington Post*, they were part of a normal family. 'I acted like their mother. I encouraged him to bring his friends home, because we wanted them to live a normal life … they ate cake and played with Legos.'[1]

---

1 Fifield, Anna. 'The Secret Life of Kim Jong Un's Aunt, Who Has Lived in the US since 1998.' *The Washington Post*, 27 May 2016, https://wapo.st/2PI7ir5.

The couple defected to the US in 1998 after the aunt's sister and the Kim children's mother, Ko Young-hui, was diagnosed with terminal breast cancer. Fearing they would lose their privileged status or worse, they fled with their own three children. Ko was receiving treatment in Switzerland at the time.

The aunt said Kim was born in 1984, a year some intelligence experts question due to its auspicious Orwellian quality. That was also the year the couple's first son was born. 'He and my son were playmates from birth, I changed both their diapers,' the aunt said. She also said that Kim arrived in Bern in 1996 when he was twelve. He was anointed his father's successor at his eighth birthday, she recalled, where he wore a general's uniform with stars and Korean generals were in attendance. (Kim's on and off sushi chef, Kenji Fujimoto, has told the same story but says it was on Kim's ninth birthday.)

There is general agreement that Kim returned to Pyongyang in 2000, where he attended the Kim Il-sung Military University from 2002–06.

80. Kim Jong-un Has Had a Long-standing Bromance with Basketball Player Dennis Rodman

Dennis Rodman is a retired professional basketball player with a notable career that put him in the National Basketball Association (NBA) Hall of Fame. Even during his playing days, his eccentric appearance helped him stand out: colourfully dyed hair, lots of tattoos and facial piercings, and torn clothing. He's dated Madonna and was once married to Carmen Electra. In recent years, he's had a well-publicised bromance with NBA superfan Kim Jong-un. He's visited Kim five times, always with a team of players for exhibition games against North Korean teams.

As a teenager, Kim followed the Chicago Bulls during the era that featured Michael Jordan and Rodman, who was the team's defensive star. Rodman first visited North Korea in 2013 upon Kim's invitation, taking along members of the Harlem Globetrotters basketball performance team. During a visit the following year, he sang 'Happy Birthday' to 'dear Jong-un' before a basketball game at Pyongyang Indoor Stadium on 8 January 2014. (We don't know if this is Kim's actual birthday since that information is strictly classified and hasn't been leaked.) You can see it here: https://youtu.be/SUxE7Dy82Pw.

Actually, it's an exaggeration to say they have a bromance. At a December 2017 appearance on *The Late Show with Stephen Colbert*, Rodman said Kim isn't his best friend and that 'For some reason, he likes me … he trusts me.' He agreed with Colbert that Kim is 'probably' a madman but insisted that in private, he is someone people can talk to and 'really wants to change his culture' but is more or less stuck with the legacy his father and grandfather left him. He ducked a question about whether he speaks Korean, or if Kim speaks English. They talk mainly about basketball, he said, adding that Kim once told him 'I don't want war.'[1] Photos show the two of them chatting through an interpreter, with Rodman wearing everything from business suits to a leather muscle vest, with his facial jewellery in plain sight, in violation of Kim's rules about dress and body piercings!

Although Rodman insists he never brings up politics with Kim, including human rights, one imprisoned American, Kenneth Bae, was released in 2014 following the birthday visit. Bae had been in a hard labour camp for two years – the longest time any American has spent in a North Korean prison – for committing 'hostile acts' against North Korea, probably related to evangelical beliefs he may have aired while leading a tour there. Bae publicly thanked Rodman for being a catalyst for his release – not for singing to Kim, but for speaking out that Bae may have done something to deserve imprisonment and inadvertently publicising his plight. (Rodman later apologised to Bae's family.) In all fairness, it should be noted that a US official was permitted to hand-deliver an appeal from President Barack Obama to Kim weeks before Bae's release.

1   What Do Dennis Rodman And Kim Jong-un Talk About? *YouTube*, 14 Dec. 2017, http://bit.ly/2BQ20Hu.

81. North Korea Holds Elections Every Five Years

North Korea holds nationwide elections every four to five years for the Supreme People's Assembly (SPA), the national legislative body, and every four years for Local People's Assemblies. Everyone over age seventeen is required to vote; refusing to do so is an act of treason. People who are immobile or ill can vote using a mobile ballot box.

The current SPA was elected in March 2014. Candidates for the 687 seats are selected by the Democratic Front for the Reunification of the Fatherland; voters merely rubber-stamp the single candidate listed on the local ballot. Kim Jong-un 'represents' his constituency, Mount Paektu, near Kim Il-sung's birthplace Mangyongdae (also called the 'sacred mountain of the Revolution'). The Kims assigned their constituencies with numbers they consider lucky. Kim Jong-un's constituency number is 111. Kim Jong-il's was 333. The numbers must work because they have been the Democratic Front's choice in every election!

The Democratic Front oversees all parties and candidates and is dominated by the Workers' Party of Korea, which holds 607 SPA seats. Here are the other election results in case you missed them:

Korean Social Democratic Party: Fifty seats. This is the successor to the Korean Democratic Party founded in 1945 by Cho Man-sik, a prominent Korean nationalist, Christian, and opponent of Kim Il-sung discussed in Fact 5.

Chondoist Chongu Party: Twenty-two seats. The Party was founded in 1946 and was actually larger than the Communist Party of Korea until it was purged in 1948.

General Association of Korean Residents in Japan: Five seats. The General Association of Korean Residents in Japan represents ethnic Koreans there who retain their

Choson nationality. They also serve as de facto emissaries there since Japan has no formal relations to North Koreans.

Religious associations: Three seats

Turnout was 99.7 per cent, according to the Inter-Parliamentary Union that tracks national parliaments in 179 countries. The near-universal turnout also provides inminbans and local authorities with a census since voting is organised by residence. It's a way to check to see if people are living in their assigned homes.

Elections to Local People's Assemblies have been held every four years since 1999. Assemblies are the administrative arms of cities, counties, and provincial areas. The total number of Assembly members depends on the population of the district they represent. The last local elections were held in June 2015 and sent 28,452 deputies to their respective chambers. The turnout rate was 99.97 per cent. All were selected by the Democratic Front and 'approved' by The People.

Voters can cross off the candidate's name printed on their ballot but must do this in full view of election officials. Some polling stations have a separate box for 'no' votes. Almost nobody dares to take this step, as it shows a lack of trust in the wisdom of those chosen by the Supreme Leader to serve. Refusing the government's choice will lead to additional surveillance, job loss, and relocation to less desirable housing.

82. Many North Koreans Believe the Kims Are Gods

North Koreans have been raised to believe that the Kims are quite literally gods endowed with otherworldly powers. 'In our collective minds,' Yeonmi Park writes, 'Kim Il Sung [sic] was our beloved grandfather and Kim Jong Il [sic] was our father.'[1] 'Mrs. Song,' one of the North Korean defectors interviewed by Barbara Demick, says that as a child, 'I lived only for Marshall Kim Il-sung and for the fatherland. I never had a thought otherwise.'[2]

North Korea's complete isolation from the rest of the world helped spread Kim Il-sung's legend and omniscient presence. Sailors claimed that stormy seas became calm when they sang songs about him. Children were taught that he made trees bloom and snow melt. Radio, and later television broadcasters, spoke of him and Kim Jong-il with the same breathlessness 'as Pentecostal preachers', Demick notes.[3]

As for his son, the official biography says a radiant star and a double rainbow greeted Kim Jong-il's birth at a secret Mount Paektu military camp while his father was fighting the Japanese. (In reality, he was born in the Soviet Union where his father was a Soviet Army officer.) And as his father is regarded as the Eternal Leader, Kim Jong-il is the Eternal Chairman. Later, Kim Jong-un's birth was said to be 'born of heaven' although this wasn't declared until he became Supreme Leader.

Modern gods need more than just the ability to control weather or seasons. Here are some of the Kim Jong-il's alleged abilities in which some North Koreans continue to believe:

---

1 Park and Vollers, *In Order to Live*, p. 47.
2 Demick, *Nothing to Envy*, p. 39.
3 Ibid., p. 45.

He walked at just three weeks old and spoke at eight weeks.

Like his father, he could control the weather.

During his three years at Kim Il-sung University, he wrote 1,500 books and composed six operas.

He created a delicacy called 'gogigyeopbbang,' double bread with meat in between. Many of us know this as a hamburger.

He played golf only once and shot 38 under par on a regulation course in Pyongyang, beating a world record and had five (some say eleven) holes-in-one. He also bowled a perfect 300 at his first try.[4]

At the 2010 World Cup, the North Korean coach told ESPN that Kim called him on an invisible cell phone he developed to give him valuable coaching advice.[5]

Kim Jong-un has also compiled a pretty impressive list of official miracles:

He won a yacht race against the CEO of a foreign yacht company at age nine.

He started driving at age three.

He climbed Mount Paektu with hundreds of fighter pilots and drank in its 'mental pabulum more powerful than any kind of nuclear weapon'.[4]

4 MSN. *Weird and wonderful claims about the North Korean Kim dynasty*. 13 March 2017, http://bit.ly/2PIyDJV.
5 Goldman, Russell. 'North Korean Soccer Coach Talks to "Dear Leader" Via Invisible Phone.' *ABC News*, 17 June 2010, https://abcn.ws/2weNYd1.

83. Kim Jong-un Harnesses Nostalgia for His Grandfather's Era

Kim Jong-un came to power at an uneasy time for North Korea. The famine was a recent memory, and much of the population was still stumbling toward a sense of normalcy. When their Great Leader died unexpectedly, he left behind a successor who had only been announced a year earlier and who many North Koreans didn't know very well.

If he were a believer, Kim must have thanked some deity for his close physical resemblance to his grandfather Kim Il-sung. He also was smart enough to realise that he'd be better off to use his natural charisma, possibly honed in Europe over video games and basketball.

Kim's first public speech occurred just a couple of months after his father's death – for whom he seems to have genuinely grieved – and on the 100th anniversary of Kim Jong-un's birth. He spoke for twenty minutes, the first time North Koreans actually heard their leader's voice in twenty years, according to the Brookings Institute's Jung H. Pak.[1] Kim Jong-il disliked public speaking and avoided it for much of his rule. But like his grandfather, Kim Il-sung enjoys meeting his people.

Kim certainly has an outgoing nature and tirelessly tours his country's worksites, schools, day-care centres and entertainment centres. He's been photographed linking arms with the people he meets and even hugs them, much as his grandfather often did. And as Pak notes, he doesn't just show up to give advice like his predecessors. He is seen

> … pulling weeds, riding roller coasters, navigating a tank, and galloping on a horse. He is comfortable with technology … and is also portrayed speaking earnestly with nuclear scientists and overseeing scores of missile tests.[1]

1 Pak, Jung H. 'The Education of Kim Jong-un.' Brookings, 20 Feb. 2018, https://brook.gs/2MARit5.

It's debatable whether Kim is trying to resemble his grandfather by putting on weight; he certainly has suffered from weight-related illnesses. If you can't walk, you can't meet the public, so maybe he's losing a few of the extra pounds.

Kim seems to really want to pull North Korea into the modern era, something his buddy Dennis Rodman has tried to convey. He's opened amusement parks, ski resorts, even skate parks – things he enjoyed himself as a teenager in Switzerland, where he skied in the Alps and visited Euro Disney. Walking around with a pretty wife clutching his arm, he gives the impression of being a bold young leader beloved by his people who are just as youthful and energetic as he.

Like his predecessors, Kim Jong-un ultimately holds onto power through fear, gulags, and executions. Opposition is not tolerated. Pak theorises that he's watched the ups and downs of dictators around the world, particularly the Arab world, and is all too aware of the brutal end met by Libya's Qadaffi.

84. Kim Jong-un's Presence Moves North Koreans to Tears

Wherever he goes, Kim Jong-un is met by sobbing citizens. His very presence moves North Koreans to tears, thanks to the personality cult his grandfather began and his father stoked.

Even when he's meeting with groups that include men, there's crying except when he's posing with his top military and political advisors – they are usually applauding and smiling and rarely look grim.

Women in particular seem to love him and are as likely to match his own wide smile as if they're meeting a rock star, although many still cry in his presence. A *New York Magazine* article titled, appropriately, 'Ladies love Cool Jong-un' shows a group of women in the jumpsuits and uniforms of the People's Army Air and Anti-Air Force surrounding Kim, who looks enormously pleased, as do the male officers in the background. All but one woman, who might be about to cry or maybe is just grimacing, are positively beaming. On one side, a woman in a flight jacket is hanging off Kim's arm while on the other side, a woman is showing him a small book – perhaps her own personal Kim scrapbook? For Kim himself, you can see the photo here: https://nym.ag/2NiRFVH.

Schoolchildren seem particularly moved to tears when they meet Kim. That's hardly surprising: from the cradle onward, they are told he's the greatest person in the world, even greater than grandma and grandpa.

Many photos of Kim with ordinary people show them reaching out to touch him, as if they believe he has healing qualities.

85. TRAFFIC LADIES MAY BE MORE ICONIC THAN THE KIMS

Although there are no badges honouring their unique place in North Korean society, it's hard to argue that Traffic Ladies are any less iconic there than the Kims. They are favourite subjects for tourist photographs because where else in the world would you find one?

Traffic Ladies, who are officially called Traffic Security Officers, do the work of traffic lights in the rest of the world. They are only in Pyongyang but it's reasonable to expect they could appear in other large cities like Hamhung and Chongjin should private cars become more common in the future.

There are around 300 such ladies in the nation's capital, says an Agence France-Presse report from the Filipino news outlet ABS-CBN, plus 400 men. Traffic Ladies are selected for their appearance and must retire at age twenty-six or when they marry, whichever comes first, because 'the role is tough and difficult' and can only be done 'when they are single' according to one officer.[1] (Traffic Men, though, are not compelled to retire because of age or marital status.)

Traffic ladies were first introduced in 1980, probably to brighten up the street scene because vehicular traffic was still pretty rare. Their uniforms are military blues, whites, or blue and white, with patrol hats that match the colour of their skirts or trousers. In nice weather, they wear knee-length skirts with white socks and black shoes with chunky heels. In the winter or when it rains, they wear dark slacks and boots. Cold-weather gear includes fur-trimmed belted overcoats and fur hats; when it's raining, they wear

---

1   Berger, Sebastien, and Agence France-Presse. 'Driven to Distraction: Pyongyang's "Traffic Ladies".' *ABS-CBN News*, 14 June 2017, http://bit.ly/2Pa6muu.

clear, full-body covers. They wear white or dark gloves depending on the season and sunglasses. They wield brightly coloured or striped batons to direct traffic and stand at attention on the sidewalk or traffic island when there is no traffic to tend to.

The current Senior Captain for Traffic Ladies (as of 2017) said the training was tough and exhausting. She practised throughout the night and kept going the next day without feeling tired thanks to 'the thought that our leader, who cares only for the happiness of our people all year long, was watching us work'.[1]

In 2013, a Traffic Lady named Ri-Kyong Sim was given North Korea's 'Hero of the Republic' medal for:

> ... ensuring the traffic order in the capital city and display[ing] the heroic self-sacrificing spirit of safeguarding the security of the headquarters of the revolution in an unexpected circumstance.

In plain language, she took action, possibly without realising it, which thwarted an assassination attempt against Kim Jong-un.[2] You can see Traffic Lady images on stamps, billboards, and posters, and buy a little Traffic Lady doll souvenir. A fan set up a website at www.pyongyangtrafficgirls.com.

2 Abad-Santos, Alexander. 'Did a Female North Korean Traffic Cop Save Kim Jong-un from Assassination?' *The Atlantic*, 30 Oct. 2013, http://bit.ly/2P7OjFx.

86. Kim Jong-un Lives a Seriously Unhealthy Lifestyle

Anyone who looks at Kim Jong-un sees a seriously overweight man and won't be surprised to read that he's had health problems.

Dr Oz would go mad over his eating and drinking habits. His diet, according to the *Los Angeles Times*, includes snake wine, which is supposed to improve virility; Hennessy; Emmenthal, a whole milk Swiss cheese; and meat pizzas. He enjoys whiskey and sushi, which he often ate with his father. Kim Jong-il also kept an Italian chef employed for his favourite son.[1]

Kim is said to have gained as much as 40 kg (88 lbs) since he took office in 2011. Some Korean experts suggest it's to make him more closely resemble his grandfather, Kim Il-sung. Here are the basics: Kim is 170 cm (5 feet 7 inches) tall, weighs around 130 kg (286 lbs), and is considered morbidly obese by US health standards. He smokes and drinks, and many observers say his face appears bloated, indicating illness, thyroid problems, or a medication side effect.[2]

In 2014, Kim was observed limping at several appearances. In July of that year, North Korean media acknowledged he'd been ill when he'd been out of sight for several weeks. There was speculation he'd been suffering from gout. More recently, in February 2018, John Pike, a military intelligence analyst who runs the website globalsecurity.org, spoke to the *Asia Times* about a photo of Kim distributed just before the Winter Olympics in South Korea. Kim appears to be supported by his sister, Kim Yo-jong, and Kim Yong-nam,

1   Rock, Taylor. 'Kim Jong Un Indulges in Expensive Booze and Meat-Covered Pizza While Country Hungers, Report Says.' *Los Angeles Times*, 3 Jan. 2018, https://lat.ms/2NqDfTk.

2   Pike, John. 'Kim Jong-un – health.' GlobalSecurity.org, Mar. 2018 http://bit.ly/2MSBcdP.

president of the Presidium of the Supreme People's Assembly, who appear to be supporting him. 'It really looks like they are holding him upright to prevent him from falling over,' Pike said. 'His face also seems rather bloated. Both of these features suggest a return of the health problems that have bedevilled him since coming to power.'[3]

Another explanation (or as we say in the US, an 'alternative fact') is that Kim was a weightlifter during his student days in Switzerland. Classmates say he loved basketball, but if he also hit the weights room there and later abruptly stopped this activity, that could result in weight gain if he didn't reduce his caloric intake.

Weightlifters need a lot of bulk to perform. Once they stop, however, muscles lose definition and the ability to burn fat. This is why so many former athletes look heavy, even if they weigh less than their 'playing' weight. Significant weight gain like Kim's happens because of a severe hormonal imbalance or thyroid problem, or, more likely, excessive eating!

Both the *Daily Mail* and *Fox News* have reported that Kim suffers from diabetes and sexually transmitted disease.

---

3 'Is Kim Jong-un Ill Again?' *Asia Times*, 14 Feb. 2018, http://bit.ly/2MC5Zfx.

87. Kim Jong-un Personally Selects Members of North Korea's Official All-female Pop Group

North Korea has an official, all-female pop group called the Moranbong Band, or sometimes the Moran Hill Orchestra. Kim Jong-un founded the band in 2012 and personally selects its members. It is part of a larger group, the Samjiyon Orchestra, which includes men and women. Moranbong Band performs only for high-profile occasions, often in Kim's presence, and at diplomatic events.

Band members are real musicians whose repertoire includes patriotic music and pop songs, including orchestral versions of the theme from *Rocky*. They sing and play symphonic and orchestral instruments as well as rock staples on keyboards, drums, and electric guitars. They perform in fashionable attire that includes dresses *well* above the knee and in high heels, and those whose instruments permit, do little dance steps. They are, apparently, the only women who can wear Western-style clothing, which is otherwise outlawed. The lead guitarist and lead singer, Hyon Song-wol, and the keyboardist have sometimes had short, nearly punky hairstyles that might not on the list of approved hairstyles discussed in Fact 48.

Performances are in front of jumbotron screens that show Kim Jong-un in various places, greeting people or leading meetings, as well as footage of missiles taking off to Japan or wherever. There's a clip on YouTube: https://youtu.be/FUjqYfyvynQ. Note the smiling snowman on the side of the stage holding a missile, the middle-aged men in dark suits standing and clapping, and the dancing women in traditional dress in front of the stage.

Sometimes the band wears uniforms – again with short skirts that other North Koran women couldn't get away with – that are a lot nicer than what real military personnel wear. In fact, each member is from the military and holds an official senior position. (They also wear sequined ball gowns and traditional Korean dress when an occasion calls for it.) According to *Time*, the band has ten–twenty members, with a fair amount of turnover. At one point, in 2013, members were put on a diet to ensure their waistlines were standardised.[1]

Being in the band has its perks. Hyon Song-wol, who is a colonel in the Korean Army, performed with the Samjiyon Orchestra in a ninety-minute show in PyeongChang, South Korea the day before the Winter Olympics opened there in 2018. She has been promoted to the Workers' Party Central Committee, *Time* says, and was at preparation talks that led to the April 2018 summit between the two Koreas.[1] In the past, there were rumours in the South Korean media that she was romantically involved with Kim Jong-un and was even executed after he married Ri Sol-ju.

The band has yet to have an international tour. A planned three-day trip to China was cancelled in 2015 after Chinese authorities objected to anti-US lyrics. The band has been called Kim's Imperial Harem on China's internet.

---

1 Meixler, Eli. 'Moranbong Band: What to Know About North Korean Girl Group.' *Time*, 16 Jan. 2018, https://ti.me/2BSkDuf.

88. NORTH KOREAN CULTURE FOSTERS LYING

A society that doesn't allow people to think for themselves doesn't encourage honesty.

Writing about her English language students at Pyongyang University of Science and Technology, Suki Kim became deeply disturbed about how easily and frequently these well-behaved and respectful young men could lie. They lied about everything from skiing (one student who said he enjoyed it could not name where he skied) to covering for those absent from class with conflicting lies. The worst part of losing a campus trivia game, one student declared, was that his team was caught cheating. They should have cheated better!

Outside of class, they pretended not to understand English-speaking instructors if they didn't want to answer a question. They lied about their own backgrounds and capabilities. One student, who had excellent English skills, claimed he only began studying the language a few months before coming to PUST, but Kim, who learned English as a second language, understood this to be virtually impossible. Yet another student told her he had cloned a rabbit.

Kim once assigned an essay on honesty and instructed her students to develop an outline. When it was due, about a quarter said they forgot to bring in their essays. She gave them permission to return to their dormitories to fetch them; only then did they admit they didn't do the work.

Interestingly, they were quick to call out perceived lies. They knew next to nothing about New York but were convinced that another teacher who mentioned ski trips in New York was lying because they 'knew' there is no snow there. In fact, New York borders Canada and has excellent ski resorts.

Sometimes students were instructed to lie, such as telling teachers they walked to downtown Pyongyang to vote when they clearly hadn't. Their primary education included falsehoods such as North Korean scientists discovering how to change blood types.

Even though there is no concept of an extended holiday in North Korea, all of Kim's students said they went home to their families in August. But she knew many remained on campus or fulfilled their national duty working on farms or at construction sites. Yet they spoke about how excited they were to see friends 'at home'. Were they pretending?

Kim theorises that living in a free society breeds trust and makes lying an exception rather than the rule. She wonders if her students really didn't understand the difference between the truth and a lie because they have been lied to all their lives. In turn, they learn to lie early on. For many, including those who escape North Korea, lying is literally a survival method. And if university students can get away with silly lies like knowing how to ski or clone animals, they may not see anything wrong about lying unless they are caught and punished. (There was no punishment for cheating on the trivia game other than disqualification.) Yet in spite of their casual lying, Kim loved her students.

89. NORTH KOREAN GRIEF OVER THE KIMS' DEATHS WAS WEIRDLY COMPETITIVE

Kim Il-sung's death in 1994 gave the world a tour de force in mourning. In spite of his advanced age (eighty-two), particularly by North Korean standards, his death was unexpected. A physician that Barbara Demick interviewed for her book recounted that even with her obvious knowledge, she somehow thought mortality didn't apply to Kim. Others talked about feeling a jolt going through their bodies when they heard the news.

What ensued, as Barbara Demick suggests, became a kind of competition about who could mourn the most and the loudest, egged on by a government propaganda machine in overdrive. North Korean television showed people beating themselves and tearing their clothes, day after day, loudly wailing that they were now fatherless, even though they were well aware that Kim Jong-il would succeed his father. Adults fainted at memorial sites, people banged their head on trees, pilots cried in their cockpits. Many of these scenes were broadcast in the West as well. 'How could you leave us so suddenly?' Demick writes one man wailed for the cameras while Pyongyang television declared 'Our country is enveloped in the deepest sorrow in the five-thousand-year history of the Korean nation.' A film was released telling people that if they cried hard enough, the cranes that descended from heaven (it apparently exists, even though the government is officially atheist) to take Kim would agree to leave him on earth.

Not everyone mourned Kim's death for real. Plenty of people admitted feeling pressured to 'grieve'. Demick writes about others who went along with the crowd lest they attract suspicion for not being sufficiently overwhelmed with grief. A university student at the prestigious Kim Chaek University of Technology found himself unable to weep although he was surrounded by sobbing classmates. Sitting with them in a communal area, he literally kept his head down and simply stared until his eyes watered. Then the environment around him took hold and he found he could cry along with the best of them.

One woman described coming home from work to find a group of people in her apartment watching her television and crying over the news. All she could think was: 'Kim Il-sung might be dead but I'm still hungry.'[1] Later, upon hearing that Kim Jong-il's succession was in place, she could only think to herself, 'Now we're really fucked.'[2]

There were similar displays of hysteria when Kim Jong-il died in 2011. Some of it could have been a real fear for the future as Kim Jong-un was barely recognisable to most North Koreans. There were scenes of people crying together in public squares, although not with quite as much of the hysteria seen in 1994. Official government statements spoke of Kim Jong-un's readiness to lead the Revolution almost as much as the Dear Leader's demise. As one cabinet member said, 'The Korean revolution is sure to always triumph under the leadership of Kim Jong-un.'

1 Demick, *Nothing to Envy*, p. 95.
2 Ibid., p. 96.

90. KIM JONG-UN'S MARCH 2018 TRIP TO BEIJING WAS HIS FIRST INTERNATIONAL TRIP AS SUPREME LEADER

Kim Jong-un's visit to Beijing in March 2018 was his first foreign trip as North Korea's Supreme Leader and came a month before his first, historic trip to South Korea. At the time of writing, he had visited Beijing three times in 2018.

As a young student in Switzerland, Kim travelled a bit through Europe with his aunt and uncle, who acted as *in loco parentis*, to go skiing, visit Euro Disney in France, and maybe take a side trip or two to Germany or Belgium. He may have visited Japan and China with his mother in the early 1990s.

The March visit was not announced until it was nearly over and was Kim's first meeting with another head of state. It came after a couple of years in which North Korea defied treaties and the United Nations to test its nuclear capabilities and delivery systems, including two that sent Hwasong-12 ballistic missiles soaring over Japan in August and September 2017. It also started quite a war of words with US President Donald Trump, who referred to Kim as 'Little Rocket Man' in an address to the UN and Kim calling Trump 'an aging dotard'.

Kim probably wanted China's buy-in for a potential visit with Trump, who tweeted an offer to meet. Plus, China's President Xi Jinping had to demonstrate his ability to manage North Korea, which had spurned his earlier approaches. Kim had also purged a lot of the old guard that were North Korea's point people in China.

When in China, do as China, and Kim pledged at a banquet that he intended to continue traditional ties with China in spite of the frosty relations that had characterised the two nations since he had come to power. For his part, Xi praised the 'promising changes in the situation on the

Korean Peninsula' over the past year, which almost sounds like an endorsement of the nuclear tests.[1] And although the trip was called unofficial, there was plenty of evidence of it in Chinese media.

It's also worth noting that earlier in the month, China's National People's Congress voted out term limits for its president just after reappointing Xi. Perhaps this swayed Kim to meet with China sooner rather than later, since it could be years until another president is appointed? All those nuclear tests cost a lot of money and China has historically been North Korea's bank, providing generous loan terms (including loan forgiveness) and expert support. But it had also backed United Nations sanctions and reduced exports, including badly needed coal, to North Korea. Kim couldn't afford to wait out xi's rule.

'At a time when the situation on the Korean Peninsula is undergoing huge unprecedented changes,' Kim echoed Xi, 'I have made this quick visit to China with the fine hopes of ... continuing and developing Korean-Chinese friendship.'[1]

---

1 Myers, Steven Lee, and Jane Perlez. 'Kim Jong-un Met With Xi Jinping In Secret Beijing Visit.' *The New York Times*, 27 Mar. 2018, https://nyti.ms/2wsJMWB.

91. No One Knows When Kim Jong-un Married Ri Sol-ju

Kim Jong-un married Ri Sol-ju on ... well, we don't know when it was because there was no public announcement. It may have been in 2009, a year before Ri had their first child. Either way, Kim was wed before he came to power in 2011 and it's a good bet that his father, Kim Jong-il, arranged it.

Part of this is cultural. North Korean weddings are low-key affairs even for the elite, and Korean parents often choose their children's spouses. When Dad is a supreme dictator, you aren't going to argue and, actually, Ri is attractive and has no doubt been prepared for her position. She is the first spouse of a North Korean leader to officially travel with her husband within the country and internationally. She accompanied Kim in March 2018 on an official visit to China and a month later to South Korea for the historic meeting between Kim and President Moon Jae-in. The Chinese really liked her and praised her on Weibo (China's version of Twitter) for her 'beautiful and amiable' appearance as well as her 'powerful presence'.[1] (Weibo can no longer mention her!)

Ri apparently was a singer and performer in the past – come to think of it, that may be how she came to Kim Jong-il's attention – and may have been a budding pop star. The government supposedly went around the country in 2012 to collect and destroy CDs and tapes that featured her performances. South Korean intelligence reports she studied singing in China and was part of North Korea's cheerleading squad when it visited South Korea in 2005 as part of a sports competition.

She would not have appeared publicly with Kim unless they were married. It would be 'unthinkable', says North Korea

---

1 Zhao, Christina. 'Kim Jong-un's Wife's Stylish Fashion Sense Is a Hit in China.' *Newsweek*, 28 Mar. 2018, http://bit.ly/2NkQ8yf.

expert Andrei Lankov, for anyone in North Korea's power structure to go out publicly with a girlfriend. 'Everything related to Kim Jong-il's children is a deadly secret,' he told CNN in 2012 shortly after the younger Kim was seen at a concert that included Disney characters with a 'mystery woman' who was later revealed to be his wife. Earlier, she had been seen walking behind Kim at a tourist site and a tribute to Kim Il-sung on the anniversary of his death. Lankov speculated that adding Ri to his public appearances was to reveal the presence of a wife given Kim's penchant at the time 'to hug everybody, physically hug'.[2]

It's been noted that Ri's three long absences from the public eye match her pregnancies; the former NBA basketball star Dennis Rodman says their second child is a girl born in 2012 or 2013. Ri is known in North Korean media as 'respected', Ri Sol-ju, the same title used for Kim's younger sister Kim Yo-jong.

2 Whiteman, Hilary. 'What Kim's "Mystery Woman" Says about North Korea.' CNN, 10 July 2012, https://cnn.it/2wpPSa5.

92. North Korean Leaders Travel in a Special Bulletproof Train

Kim Jong-un travelled by train for his first trip to China as Supreme Leader, using his father's preferred way to travel. His train, which is probably the same one his father used, is a bit different than British Rail trains. It's actually a three-train caravan, which travels together, and totals ninety carriages. A lead convoy provides reconnaissance and makes sure tracks ahead are safe, while the last one provides security. Valuable cargo is in the middle train.

Each carriage is bulletproof, making them several times heavier than standard ones. All this weight keeps the speed limited to around 60 km an hour (37 mph). On board, there are flat-screen TVs, satellite phones, bedrooms, and we can assume a full gourmet kitchen to serve up sushi, pizza, Danish pork, perhaps Kobe burgers topped with Emmenthal – whatever the Supreme Leader craves. Kim has been filmed meeting with staff in the same dining car/conference room his father used, with a MacBook at his side. There's also a lounge room lined with comfy-looking red leather sofas and chairs where Kim, Ri, and their entourage were photographed and filmed en route to Beijing.

Kim's father reportedly ensured the train had a full complement of cuisines – Korean, Russian, Japanese, French, and Chinese – according to memoirs by Russia's General Konstantin Pulikovsky, who accompanied Kim Jong-il to Russia in 2001. Pulikovsky described meals served with silver chopsticks, cases of Burgundy and Bordeaux wines flown in from France, live lobsters, and entertainment from 'beautiful lady conductors' who sang old Soviet-era songs.[1] Kim Jong-il used the train extensively for travel throughout

---

1   Brooke, James. 'A Telling North Korean Journey.' *The New York Times*, 3 Dec. 2002, https://nyti.ms/2MDADp6.

North Korea and even had around twenty railroad stations constructed for his exclusive use.

Unlike his father and grandfather, Kim Jong-un has no qualms about air travel and is said to have a strong interest in aircraft and aerospace. North Korean media have shown him flying a small aircraft, and he seems to understand the panels before him in photos where he's seated in military cockpits. He flew to China for his second visit in May 2018 aboard a Soviet-made Ilyushin-62 passenger jet, which might be part of the fleet he uses for interior travel, and where he has been photographed holding meetings. This trip, to the north-eastern Chinese city of Dalian, known for its Yellow Sea beaches, ended with Kim and Xi pledging to formally end the Korean War and denuclearise the peninsula. From there, Kim went on to meet with President Trump in Singapore.

Kim also flew to China for his third visit in June 2018, a post-Trump official trip where he was met by his own $1 million armoured Mercedes-Benz stretch limo. Kim and Xi repeated the denuclearisation pledge, but gave no timeframe. With US sanctions looming, China may have wanted to demonstrate its continued influence over North Korea, while Kim, at last, got his official visit as a head of state.

93. Plastic Surgery is Common among the Higher Songbun

During her tenure teaching English in Pyongyang, Suki Kim noticed during her trips into the city that many women looked as if they'd had blepharoplasty, better known as double-eyelid surgery. This surgery, which inserts a crease in the eyelid to make the eyes look larger, is the most common kind of surgery in South Korea. Although eyelid surgery was initially controversial, it's now widespread across Asia, particularly among teenagers and young people, and men are as likely as women to get it.

Kim's students (at the time, PUST only accepted men) told her that plastic surgery was almost standard among women in North Korea and several mentioned sisters who had had it. As they were mostly from the higher songbun, this isn't terribly surprising. Kim had also heard from a colleague that local women could receive plastic surgery as a kind of reward from the government.[1]

North Koreans want plastic surgery for the same reason most people do for non-medical reasons: to improve their appearance, at least in their own eyes. Large eyes, it seems, are now universally attractive: young people, including North Koreans, say having the surgery will help them advance. In North Korea, this can mean better jobs, housing, and the opportunity to work abroad.

According to a 2006 article from the South Korean online paper *Daily NK*, eyelid surgery and eyebrow tattooing (not an actual surgery) was already well established in Shinuiju, one of the smuggling centres in the northern part of North Korea just across the Yalu River from Dandong, China. Sixty per cent of women there have had one or both of

1   Kim, *Without You There is No Us,* p. 254.

these procedures.[2] The government doesn't approve, a local 'trader' told the paper, but it's so popular that it's reluctant to crack down.

As we say in the US, there's a new sheriff in town, and he's not cracking down on legal or illegal plastic surgery. In fact, North Koreans who have had plastic surgery openly discuss it, according to an exposé from *Daily NK*. And while plastic surgery is not a speciality in North Korea, plenty of surgeons perform the procedures, and there are many unlicensed private, or 'house', practitioners as well.[3]

Which begs the question: did Kim Jong-un enhance his features to resemble his grandfather? The North Korean media were furious when this was reported in the Chinese press and picked up by South Korea in 2013. It all seems unlikely; Kim doesn't look all that different from when he first appeared on the scene in 2010 other than the notable weight gain. He certainly doesn't have the same hairstyle as his grandfather, and who can blame him for preferring tailored suits to his father's safari wear?

2 '60 per cent of Single Women in Shinuiju Get Plastic Surgery on Their Eyelids.' *Daily NK*, 10 May 2006, http://bit.ly/2Mxqn1s.
3 'Plastic Surgery Demands Heat up This Summer. *Daily NK*, 24 Aug. 2015, http://bit.ly/2BNHpmQ.

94. NORTH KOREANS COLLECT THEIR FAECES TO CONTRIBUTE TO AN IMPORTANT NATIONAL RESOURCE

North Korea is so desperate for fertilizer it requires citizens to collect their own faeces, supplemented with animal output if necessary, to contribute to a national effort. This is the 'night soil' referenced in Fact 23.

Even devoted Korea-watchers missed this one (or at least didn't discuss it) until Yeonmi Park published her memoir about surviving the famine, escaping to China and eventually getting to South Korea. It seems the Soviet Union stopped sending fertilizer to North Korea around 1990, so, in the spirit of Juche, the people stepped in. South Korea used to send fertilizer as well as part of an anti-famine measure. That ended when the North sank one of its ships in 2010.

Everyone, children included, has a quota they must (literally) fill. This was not as easy as you might think during a famine. Park, who briefly lived with relatives, remembers being told not to poop at school: 'Wait to do it here!' One aunt used to complain that she kept forgetting to take plastic bags with her whenever she travelled so she could save her, uh, output. "Next time I'll remember!" Park recounts she would pledge. 'Thankfully, she never did.'[1]

Things got so bad, Park says, that people started locking their outhouses to prevent stealing. (Most families, particularly outside the major cities, do not have indoor plumbing.) School would be halted to send children out to collect dog waste; 'if you saw a dog pooping in the street, it was like gold.'[1] One uncle had a big dog; family members would fight to collect its donations.

Kim Jong-un didn't exactly order the continuation of this effort. He did suggest in 2014, as part of the famous

---

1 Park, *In Order to Live*, p. 89.

'advice' all Kims provide during official trips to farms and factories, to collect animal waste to build up the national fertilizer supply. Apparently this was already a practice at many farms; according to Lee Min-bok, an agriculturist who defected to South Korea in 1995, farmers were already using 'night soil'. Furthermore, 'vegetables grown in it are considered more delicious than others', he told Reuters.[2]

Wealthier families who can avoid the collection bucket buy their donations from ranches. It wouldn't be surprising to find a black market for this resource too.

The fertilizer solution has, unfortunately, brought on more misery in an already miserable health system. It's led to more parasites and is even affecting military personnel, as noted in Fact 30.

It is not known if Kim Jong-un donates. If he doesn't, that's a sadly wasted resource. It's been pretty widely reported that he travels with a personal portable toilet to ensure physicians monitor his output. He's understandably concerned about poisoning and also doesn't want enemies or foreign intelligence to get hold of his biologics.

---

2 Smith, Josh. 'Injured Defector's Parasites and Diet Hint at Hard Life in North Korea.' *Reuters*, 17 Nov. 2017, https://reut.rs/2MVrpDE.

95. Twins and Triplets in North Korea Are Raised Away from Their Families

Infant triplets born in North Korea, and many sets of twins as well, are removed from their families and sent to orphanages, presumably to spare the parents the cost of raising so many children. Trips to see 'lucky' triplets appear on tourist itineraries, including that of Wendy E. Simmons, who took a photojournalist approach to document her visit to North Korea.

'Twins and triplets are a big deal in North Korea,' she writes in her book *My Holiday in North Korea: The Funniest/Worst Place on Earth*. 'Families are accorded certain privileges' that include extra milk per child during pregnancy and round-trip helicopter flights for mothers from their homes anywhere in the countryside to Pyongyang Women's Hospital. Upon their children's birth, parents receive gold rings or daggers[1] – and then the children are removed, often right away. Elite families can keep their children until around age two, according to an account published in *The Sunday Times*.

This practice is an unfortunate result of food aid given to North Korea during the 1990s famine. It gave the Kims the opportunity to take advantage of numerology beliefs regarding the power of the number 3 and perhaps, as Simmons speculates, keep triplets under tight state control lest 'today's baby triumvirate' becomes 'tomorrow's defenestration.'[2]

Her orphanage visit featured the same Spartan surroundings other have reported, particularly for the infants. The toddlers she met were cute and looked healthy

1 Simmons, W. E., *My holiday in North Korea: The Funniest/Worst Place on Earth* (NY: Rosetta Books, 2016), p. 129.
2 Ibid, p. 130

and eager to sing for her. Her photos show sets of twins and triplets dressed in matching outfits.

Asked about the policy of separating triplets from families, North Korea told the UN Human Rights Commission:

> Triplets are supplied by the state free of charge with clothing, bedding, a one-year supply of dairy products and a pre-school subsidy, and special medical workers take charge of such mothers and children and care for their health.[3]

The Korean Friendship Association, a propaganda arm that runs North Korea's official website, reported on 'talented triplets' who sang in Pyongyang 'on the occasion of the New Year Juche 103 or 2014'. The article took pains to highlight the 'special treatment and meticulous care' the children received in 'a baby home at state expense under the nursing system of the state'. Their parents, an army officer and a cobbler, were given 'various kinds of tonics, daily necessities, and nice houses'. Their mother echoed these praises.[4]

In 2015, the UPI news service reported an 'unprecedented number of triplet births' and a cause of celebration given the country's low birth rate.[5]

---

3 Michael Sheridan. 'Kim kidnaps Korea's "lucky" triplets.' *The Sunday Times*, 9 March 2003. Retrieved from http://bit.ly/2PFNAwl.
4 'Triplets Develop Their Talents.' Retrieved from http://bit.ly/2MSDg5z.
5 Shim, E. 'North Korea claims baby boom in triplets.' UPI, 17 June 2015. http://bit.ly/2nPRXby

96. North Korean Scientists Found a Unicorn Lair

The Korean Central News Agency announced in 2012 that archaeologists from the History Institute of the Academy of Social Sciences had discovered a unicorn lair north of Pyongyang.

Actually, the scientists found a kirin lair. The news agency mistranslated the discovery into 'unicorn', but that's semantics for you. Kirin are mythical beasts with the body of a deer, tail of a cow, hooves, and a mane, plus a single horn growing from its head. They originated in China, where they are called 'Chinese unicorns' or 'qilin,' and are popular features in Eastern art. In Japan, they are called kirin, which also translates into 'giraffe' and is the name of a very nice beer.

Anyway, the discovery of the kirin lair was taken to be evidence that Pyongyang is an ancient capital. The lair belonged to King Dongmyong (also called Jumong), who founded the Go Dynasty and the Goguryeo Kingdom, one of the Three Kingdoms of Korea. The name Goguryeo was later shortened to Goryeo, which is the origin of the English word for Korea.

Dongmyong, who lived from 37–19 BCE, was the son of a 'heavenly prince' and a woman who was the daughter of the god of the Yellow River. The Go Dynasty lasted more than 700 years. Its founder remains a popular mythological hero in Korea and is strongly associated with kirin, his favourite way to travel.

Dongmyong was deified after his death and worshipped at a magnificent temple that still stands within Pyongyang. His descendants carry the surname Go.

97. Outsiders Conduct Air Drops of DVDs, Bibles, and Food Wrappers into North Korea

Lots of stuff falls from North Korean skies near the southern border. Fighters for a Free North Korea (http://www.rokdrop.net/tag/fighters-for-a-free-north-korea/) is probably the best known of the handful of active South Korean airdrop groups. Over the years, the group has sent the following items into North Korea via helium balloons and possibly drones:

Human rights and pro-democracy literature

Transistor radios

USB flash drives and SD cards loaded with information about life in South Korea as well as movies and TV shows

DVDs, particularly documentaries and the 2015 movie *The Interview*

Fighters for a Free North Korea is chaired by a refugee named Park Sang-hak, who grew up in a privileged North Korean family but was inspired by his Japanese grandmother who told him about the outside world and life without an inminban. A graduate of the elite Kim Chaek University, he defected with his parents and siblings using false passports. (Songbun status has its additional privileges.) Park was also the target of two foiled assassination attempts. One, ironically, was from another North Korean defector.

In 1991, a group of evangelical Christians began printing Bible verses in Korean onto orange helium balloons, which it releases near the DMZ into North Korea. The group is still going strong. 'By sending these balloons, we let our North Koran brothers and sisters know that we are praying for them and the scriptures on the balloons are meant to encourage them,' one activist told *CBN News*.[1] In the past, the group also used boats to launch larger balloon packages from the Sea of Japan/East Sea and the Yellow Sea that contained additional Biblical and New Testament literature, and transistor radios.

In 2014, news came out that the North Korean regime cracked down on smuggled snacks, particularly something called Choco Pies that were given as perks to North Koreans working in South Korean factories in Kaesong. In response, 200 sympathetic activists gathered in the border city of Paju and released 500 large, condom-shaped helium balloons carrying 770 Ibs of different snack foods including 10,000 Choco Pies.

Other groups airdrop hard currency, usually US dollars. One man sends empty food wrappers to show North Koreans what they are missing. Activists in the border region have been known to stand in the Bukhan, or North Han, River and throw packages across it to North Koreans. For this reason, North Korean soldiers in the area are instructed to shoot people with wet clothing or hair because they are probably carrying contraband.

Former US Navy SEAL Jocko Willink suggested dropping 25 million iPhones and launching satellites over North Korea for free Wi-Fi.[2] It's intriguing, especially since China makes fewer parts for Apple these days.

1 Thomas, George. 'Bible "Balloon Offensive" Floats into North Korea.' CBN.com, 15 Aug. 2017, http://bit.ly/2NoQjsD.
2 Willink, Jocko. 'Drop 25 Million IPhones on Them and Put Satellites over Them with Free WiFi.' Twitter, 7 Sept. 2017, http://bit.ly/2MSWQie.

98. Grain Is Scarce in North Korea, so Alcohol is Made from Acorns

Grain is scarce in North Korea, even without the usual famines, floods, and droughts. As the famine wore on, Kim Jong-il decided that grain and maize, which had been used to make alcohol, needed to be preserved for eating. This put breweries and home brewers in quite a bind until they turned to a more readily available tannin and brewing source: acorns from North Korea's once-abundant oak trees.

A lot of alcohol in North Korea is brewed from acorns. It's so popular that the average person can actually barter acorns with their local distillery. But now there is an acorn shortage and recent satellite images show a great deal of tree loss, possibly because people cut them down to use for firewood during energy shortages.

Even during a famine, rice remains a staple and its harvesting is a huge priority; there are reports of soldiers taking over the rice harvest when farmers became too weak from malnutrition to do so. Rice is also used to make soju, a clear liquor that can be made from any available grain or starch. Rice soju is the drink of choice for most non-elite North Koreans.

Soju is also the base for other liquors, some of which are pretty exotic to Western palates. Bem ju, for example, is made when a snake is put in a jar of Soju or other distilled liquor. It began as a folk remedy to cure impotence, or as they say in the United States, 'low testosterone'. Andrei Lankov writes its alcohol content is 60 per cent, which will probably kill anything that stands in its way.[1] Some distillers use ants instead of snakes and if this freaks you out, you should know that The Cambridge Distillery, the 'world's first Gin Tailor', gathers red ants from Kent to brew in Grantchester.

1 Lankov, *North of the DMZ*, 2007, p. 101.

Older Koreans tend to prefer medicinal rice wines, or bek se ju. These are served in restaurants, infused with ginseng (isanju), ginger, liquorice, cinnamon and other spices. Grapes grow in the northern part of the country but they aren't very good and wines derived from grapes aren't all that popular.

Beer is not particularly popular either, probably because it's not native to Korea; Europeans introduced it there and the government used to run beer halls in major cities. Beer is available in restaurants, particularly those that cater to tourists. There are rumours of a microbrewery in the North that brews a nice stout.

There are distilleries that produce spirits for the elite and for special occasions for the less elite such as weddings. To get these treats, North Koreans fill out an application form that requires proof of the event; red tape flourishes in the most unlikely places. Still, the limit is just five bottles per event, so most of the non-elite get their booze from other sources, such as 'Halmeoni's' (Grandmother's) kitchen.

99. Even North Korea Has a Housing Market

Most North Korean housing is grim if accounts by defectors and photos sneaked out of the country are anything to go by. Yeonmi Park and Lucia Jang both grew up without running water (they used outhouses) and unpredictable electricity.

Pyongyang housing is dingy if spacious. Flats are around 100m² (1,076 ft²) and devoid of everyday luxuries including reliable electricity, according to research from 'Teoalida's Website', which features housing information on several Far East nations. As Teoalida notes, the lack of electricity is a real problem because many apartment homes are twenty to forty stories high, a lot of stairs to climb![1] Eric Lafforgue's photos of older apartment buildings show stained and crumbling concrete boxes.[2] Outside Pyongyang, homes often lack basic plumbing and electricity. Lafforgue's photos show brick and concrete homes with uneven rooftops lining unpaved roads.[2]

In 2014, North Korea made a rare admission that something went wrong. A twenty-three-storey apartment building collapsed, killing at least thirty people and perhaps as many as 100. Ninety-two families, including high-ranking members of the Workers' Party, lived in the building, which was not yet complete. The collapse was blamed on shoddy construction and materials; quality materials are often sold on the black market and replaced with flimsy substitutes. Kim forced senior officials to

---

1 Teoalida. 'Housing in North Korea (and Life inside Country).' Teoalida Website, 22 June 2018, http://bit.ly/2ocSMLD.

2 Styles, Ruth. 'Haunting Pictures inside North Korea ... Taken by a Photographer Who Has Now Been Banned from the Rogue State for Life.' *Daily Mail Online*, 9 May 2014, https://dailym. ai/2nLj5bF.

publicly apologise – very rare in North Korea – and later executed four of them. The military official in charge of the project was sent to a prison camp.

North Koreans do not own their homes but are assigned to them; the higher one's Juche status, the better the home. Legally, homes are not theirs to sell or rent. However, many people trade or sell their residency certificates, apparently with the approval of local governments, which issue new residency certificates after a sale. *NK News* reported in 2016 that the most desirable homes outside Pyongyang were near railroad stations; those near major roads can also command a nice pile of won. Inside Pyongyang, the most desirable flats are those built within the past twenty-five years because they have hot water and private bathrooms and can fetch as much as $100,000 (£77,000).[3]

Home prices on both sides of the Yalu River soared in 2018 thanks to Kim's three visits to China this year (as of press time). Chinese buyers are particularly interested in North Korean properties. Teoalida told me that the website has been getting queries from Americans interested in buying North Korean properties. The real estate boom has also created a market for home interiors aside from the obligatory placement of Kim Il-sung and Kim Jong-il portraits.

3 Lankov, Andrei. '"Owning" a Home in North Korea.' *NK News*, 2 June 2018, http://bit.ly/2PIjPes.

100. THE US–NORTH KOREAN SUMMIT LAID OUT 'BABY STEPS'

Kim Jong-un and Donald Trump met for perhaps two hours in June 2018 in Singapore. Given Trump's inattention to detail and facts, it's safe to say his staff laid out the agreement. It amounts to baby steps, which is probably the most realistic way to begin a new relationship.

Just before the summit, Trump gave North Korea a huge present by announcing a halt to annual military exercises with South Korea. At the time of writing, joint US–South Korea military exercises appeared to have been cancelled for at least one year.

Here are the terms the two countries agreed to:

Establish new relations toward peace and prosperity

Build a lasting and stable peace on the Korean Peninsula

Reaffirm denuclearisation of the peninsula, agreed to at the inter-Korean summit

Recover and repatriate Korean War remains of US prisoners of war and those missing in action

No timelines were set for these actions. Trump called the document 'very comprehensive'. Judge for yourself: it's at http://bit.ly/2nFwa6o.

Kim handled Trump well. He arrived at the summit before Trump, a courtesy that probably pleased him. Afterward, Trump burbled on about Kim's 'great personality' and how 'he loves his country and wants to do good by them'. Trump sidestepped questions from Voice of America (a news outlet administered by the US government) about starvation and brutality in North Korea and insisted he could only 'go by today and yesterday and a couple of weeks ago because that's when this whole thing started'.[1]

North Korea has returned remains from the war. In the past, some repatriated remains have been found to be from animals. Laboratory officials who examined remains returned in August 2018 say they are consistent with 'being Americans'.[2] They were returned with military equipment used by US forces during the war.[2]

North Korea has kept its word to shut down Punggye-ri, its main nuclear test site and where all six recent tests were conducted. Satellite images show key operational buildings were torn down and a railroad line to one of the facility's entrances has been removed, a good indicator of 'evidence of an operational shutdown', the website 38 North reported in May 2018. The two largest buildings at the Command Centre and Main Administrative Support Area are still intact, but that may be because journalists will witness its final dismantling – complete with explosions and tunnel collapses.[3] It would be ideal if UN experts could visit the site to verify its decommissioning but North Korea is not party to treaties that require this.

1 Susteren, Greta Van. Trump to VOA: 'We're Going to Denuke North Korea.' VOA, 13 June 2018, http://bit.ly/2NokD6F.

2 Burns, Robert. 'Remains from North Korea "Consistent With Being Americans".' *Time*, 2 Aug. 2018, https://ti.me/2BYHCDM.

3 Madden, Michael. 'North Korea Has Begun Dismantlement of the Punggye-ri Nuclear Test Site–38 North: Informed Analysis of North Korea., 14 May 2018, http://bit.ly/2PG8NGv.